The Grammar Bo

Other titles from Bloomsbury Education

100 Ideas for Primary Teachers: Literacy by Rob Smith and Katherine Simpson
100 Ideas for Primary Teachers: Writing by Adam Bushnell, Rob Smith and David Waugh
How to be an Outstanding Primary Middle Leader by Zoë Paramour
Igniting Children's Writing by Mark McCaughan
Let's Perform: Monologues, duologues and poems for children to perform by Cath Howe
Teaching for Mastery in Writing by Mike Cain
Vocabulary Ninja by Andrew Jennings

The Grammar Book

Understanding and teaching primary grammar

By Zoë and Timothy Paramour

BLOOMSBURY EDUCATION

LONDON   OXFORD   NEW YORK   NEW DELHI   SYDNEY

BLOOMSBURY EDUCATION
Bloomsbury Publishing Plc
50 Bedford Square, London, WC1B 3DP, UK

BLOOMSBURY, BLOOMSBURY EDUCATION and the Diana logo are
trademarks of Bloomsbury Publishing Plc

First published in Great Britain, 2020

A catalogue record for this book is available from the British Library

ISBN: PB: 978-1-4729-7229-3; ePDF: 978-1-4729-7228-6;
ePub: 978-1-4729-7230-9

2 4 6 8 10 9 7 5 3 1 (paperback)

Typeset by Newgen KnowledgeWorks Pvt. Ltd., Chennai, India
Printed and bound in the UK by CPI Group (UK) Ltd., Croydon CR0 4YY

To find out more about our authors and books visit www.bloomsbury.com
and sign up for our newsletters

For Bubbles, the cat with no eyebrows.

Contents

Acknowledgements

Writing a book can be a very isolating endeavour. Even writing as co-authors requires hours of work alone, at a computer. Luckily, we have some wonderful people around us who seem to tolerate us rambling on about grammar, way past the point of them losing interest.

Timothy

I want, first and foremost, to thank Hannah Marston, our fantastic editor. I'd also like to thank all those people alongside whom I have battled grammar issues in schools, including everyone at Chorleywood, Holly Park and North Harringay, and especially Steve Baptiste, Kathy Noble, Jane Alexander, Emma Hassan and David Joyce. I also want to thank Joe Layburn and everyone who has taught English at Bancroft's over the last two years, especially Alex Adams, Clive Pearson, Nick Thomas and Sarah Strong. I need to give a special mention to my sister, Alexandra, whose help and advice on grammatical matters have been invaluable. Finally, of course, I need to thank my wife, Zoë. If our love can survive writing a book about grammar together, it can survive anything.

Zoë

Thank you to Hannah for listening politely when we pitched this idea way back in 2018. It has, once again, been a real pleasure working with you. Thank you for your support and belief in us – and for fielding endless questions. I would also like to thank Caroline Spencer, Vicky Bingham and Lucy Szemerenyi for their endless support with this project and for encouraging me to speak out. Thanks to the staff at South Hampstead – working with you continues to be a privilege. Thanks to GMF for providing the wine. I would also like to thank Kath Shaw for being my fellow grammar geek for over a decade now and for proofreading and editing my tweets. And finally, thanks to my husband, Tim. We often joked that writing this book was a test of our marriage. If that is true, we have passed with flying colours, although it will be quite nice to have a summer holiday where we don't discuss the conventions of adjuncts. Here's to our next adventure.

Introduction

Ms Armstrong doesn't look worried. She rarely does. She's several years into her second successful headship; she's battled budget cuts and political change, and her staff are rightly confident in her. And maybe she isn't worried exactly, but she's certainly feeling a little out of her depth. This afternoon she's attending a meeting with her school's senior and middle leaders, where the English coordinator will unveil the new grammar scheme of work. Having had a quick flick through its pages, Ms Armstrong is aware that she isn't familiar with many of the words and phrases in the document, especially those at the top end of Key Stage 2: *coordinating conjunction, subjunctive mood, past progressive tense*. Ms Armstrong didn't learn about any of this when she was younger. She went to school in the seventies and eighties and she mostly remembers her English teachers being brilliant, but they taught her to write by exposing her to examples of writing, and most of her understanding of grammar, which she rightly believes to be pretty good, was absorbed by osmosis. She *feels* where the commas should go in a sentence and she usually gets it right – but she can't necessarily explain how or why using technical linguistic terms. She's always been an avid reader and a very competent writer. All the grammar stuff on the primary curriculum now just seems so... unnecessary. She says nothing but silently curses Michael Gove.

In a classroom on the floor above, learning support assistant Mr Yildiz has just been handed next week's English planning by the Year 6 class teacher. On Wednesday, he has to take a group of children 'who are struggling to identify the subject and object in a sentence' out of class and help them. There's just one problem and you can probably guess what it is: Mr Yildiz has no idea how to identify the subject and object in a sentence. He went to school in the nineties and noughties, when the National Literacy Strategy reigned supreme. His English lessons were rather more prescriptive and content-driven than Ms Armstrong's had been 20 years before but the content still seemed to be different from what children are learning now. Mr Yildiz and his family moved to Britain from Turkey when he was four years old and he can see some logic in teaching grammar discretely. He often used to make mistakes with verb tenses that would never cause problems for native English speakers. His teachers would circle or underline them but they rarely explained *why* they were wrong. Even now, he can still make these mistakes if he's not careful and it's really embarrassing. Mr Yildiz wants to do his PGCE next year and become a teacher but he's worried that his colleagues will think he isn't clever enough.

Down the road, Mrs Patterson is helping her ten-year-old son with his English homework. A word in a sentence has been underlined and he has to state whether it's a determiner, a pronoun or a preposition. Mrs Patterson has been googling all three words for half an hour to try to come up with an answer and she thinks she might be getting somewhere. It's certainly not the most baffling task he's come home with this year; a fortnight ago he'd had this piece of work to do about *main and subordinate clauses,* and before half-term there was that bewildering activity on *fronted adverbials.* Ironically, Mrs Patterson voted for this. The government said that they were going to bring 'rigour' back to the education system and it had sounded great. She thought she wanted her children to have a proper, traditional education, but this isn't quite what she was expecting.

Ms Armstrong, Mr Yildiz and Mrs Patterson, as you've probably guessed, are fictional characters, but that doesn't mean they aren't real. Or, at least, the grammar demons that haunt them are as real as can be and they are currently on the rampage in school communities across England. The frustration and irritation felt by Ms Armstrong, the fear and embarrassment felt by Mr Yildiz and the utter bewilderment felt by Mrs Patterson are all understandable and reasonable responses to a rapid and radical change of emphasis in the English curriculum over the course of the last decade. We've faced the grammar demons ourselves and, like most adults of working age in this country, we weren't taught grammar formally when we were at school. But we defeated our grammar demons and we wrote this book because we want to help you to defeat yours.

What's changed?

In the time we have been teaching, we have seen dramatic changes to the English curriculum. We both joined the profession in the shadow of the 'National Literacy Hour' – if you look carefully you may still find the ring binders at the back of a dusty cupboard in your school. This was an attempt to break down the English curriculum into teachable chunks. However, a lot of grammar was oversimplified to the point that teachers did not always fully understand what they were teaching. The term 'connectives' is a hangover from this era (see page 111 for the problems with connectives). It became clear that this was over-prescriptive and was often limiting more experienced teachers, and the 'National Literacy Hour' ended up being phased out in the late noughties.

With less prescription in the curriculum itself, schools and primary teachers entered a period where what they were expected to teach became synonymous with what was being assessed. 'Assessing Pupil Progress' (APP) grids were produced, outlining what 'good writing' (and sometimes, confusingly, bad writing) should look like for children working at the different levels of the old National Curriculum assessment system. This sometimes made it hard for schools to make effective judgements about what needed to be taught when in terms of grammar and punctuation. This was the background to the reforms that created the current system.

The National Curriculum changed radically in 2014 and statutory assessments changed more gradually in the years before and after the new curriculum was introduced. Both now reflect a greater emphasis on the discrete teaching of grammatical terms as a way to understand and talk about language. The way in which this has been done is far from perfect and, throughout this book, we will explore some of the issues that we still don't think the Department for Education has got quite right. However, it's where we are now, whether we like it or not, and we think that it's best to avoid the rose-tinted spectacles. We didn't live in a utopia as far as English teaching was concerned before the grammar, punctuation and spelling test was introduced and, with the right approach, we don't have to resign ourselves to living in a dystopia now. We can do all the things we, as teachers, believe in; we can teach our children to write with flair and individuality and deliver the requirements of the curriculum. In fact, a genuinely good understanding of the foundations of grammar should actually help with all of this.

Who are we?

Other than self-confessed grammar geeks and demon defeaters, who are we and why are we writing this book?

Well, we are Zoë and Timothy Paramour. At present, we are both class teachers and English coordinators in our respective schools. We have almost 25 years' combined experience of teaching and leading in primary schools. We've both held a variety of roles, from NQT to SLT, and, between us, we have worked under 15 different headteachers, three Ofsted frameworks and several revisions of the National Curriculum – that's a lot of change!

Throughout our careers, we have been interested in educational research, developing our subject knowledge and pedagogy, and we both harboured not-so-secret dreams of being writers when we were growing up. Over the years, we gradually managed to merge our two passions and started writing about education. Timothy blogs about education at https://timparamour. com and has written a play about the British education system, *Finding Mr Paramour*. Zoë blogs at 'The Girl on the Piccadilly Line' (https://piclinegirl.com) and has also written another book for Bloomsbury Education about middle leadership in a primary school. (It's more entertaining than it sounds, we promise.)

As you have probably clocked from the surnames, we are married, or at least we are as we start the long process of writing this book. Who knows where we will be after 18 months of grappling with the intricacies of English grammar?

The grammar demons

The grammar demons are not creatures of flesh and blood; they exist in our minds. However, the beings who put them there are very real and unfortunately you'll find them in most schools. They are the grammar pedants – those people who think they know all the 'rules' and 'right answers' when it comes to grammar and who like nothing more than to correct others when they believe they are violating these 'rules'. They sound terribly clever and they can make all your irritation, fear and confusion about grammar immeasurably worse. They like to tell people when they should use *whom* as opposed to *who*. They like to tell people that you can't end a sentence with a preposition. And they really like to tell people that you can't begin a sentence with *and* or *but*. But the grammar pedants don't know what they're talking about. When a grammar pedant tells you that you *can't* do this or you *must* do that, you should always feel entitled to ask them why or why not. Their response will usually be somewhat circular. 'It's against the rules,' they might say. This is not a satisfactory response. The grammar pedant is a fraud. Ms Armstrong, Mr Yildiz and Mrs Patterson shouldn't fear him or her. To understand why, we need to talk about rules.

There are two types of rule. Firstly, there are universal rules that we observe in the world and that we are powerless to change, like the rules of mathematics or the laws of physics. Grammar certainly can't be governed by these sorts of rules – languages were invented by people and they change over the years. Secondly, there are man-made rules whereby someone in authority enforces regulations on those under their jurisdiction. National laws and school codes of conduct are examples of this type of rule. But who has authority over the English language? Who is in charge of it and who has the right to create rules about how it can be used? The answer surely is no one. So, if there are no natural, universal laws governing grammar and there is no one in charge of the English language making human rules, we are left with an inescapable but surprising conclusion: grammar doesn't have rules.

So, if grammar doesn't have rules, what does it have? If a child in your class uses *your* when most educated English speakers would use *you're*, what's your basis for correcting them? The answer is simple. To say that the spelling choice is 'wrong' is merely a shorthand for saying it's 'not what most people do'. Shared norms about how we communicate ensure that we make ourselves understood. English wasn't designed. It developed and evolved over millennia. It wasn't constructed according to any rules – it just happened. Grammar is the way that we analyse the big, chaotic, random thing we call the English language and try to explain how it works. It's sometimes clumsy and imperfect – and for almost any generalisation you can make about English grammar, there will be exceptions. Grammar is not a means for *regulating* how people *should* speak and write. It is a way of *describing* how people *do*, in fact, speak and write. For that reason, you will notice throughout this book that we avoid the word *rule* and we avoid prescriptive verbs such as *should, must* or *can't* when describing the conventions of grammar. Doctors prescribe medication to patients who need it and they need to be qualified to do so. Grammar pedants are the self-appointed doctors of the English language but they have no qualifications. Beware their snake oil prescriptions.

Conventions: acceptable and unacceptable grammar

The closest we will come to being prescriptive in this book is when we talk about <u>acceptable</u> and <u>unacceptable</u> constructions. Consider these two sentences:

    I like football.
    ~~**Like I football.**~~

The first of these is grammatically acceptable and the second is not. Throughout the book, we will strike through all examples of unacceptable constructions to avoid confusion. What makes it unacceptable? We know by now that it isn't breaking a rule. So what's unacceptable about it? The issue is one of <u>convention</u>. When saying or writing this sort of sentence, English speakers tend to put the subject (I) before the verb (like). It's just what they do. The first one is the acceptable version simply because we all accept that it is. I know it and you know it – it's acceptable because we accept it! Almost anyone would think the second one looked odd and almost anyone would find it harder to understand. It's not violating any regulations and it's not breaking the laws of physics but it simply doesn't conform to our agreed sense of how English works. It just *looks wrong*.

The example above is an obvious one but there are greyer areas. Consider these two examples:

Clive has fewer sweets than Alex.
~~**Clive has less sweets than Alex.**~~

Is it true that the second of these sentences *looks wrong* to all English speakers? No. However, it does *look wrong* to enough people that it's probably worth avoiding. If you're not sure about the distinction between *less* and *fewer*, you might want to read the section on countable and uncountable nouns in Chapter 2, page 26. Exactly where the line is between acceptable and unacceptable grammar is not always clear. In this book, for example, we take the view that using *less* in place of *fewer* is generally unacceptable but using *who* in place of *whom* is generally acceptable. Like so much in grammar, that's an opinion, not a fact. You will read other books by other authors who draw their lines between the acceptable and the unacceptable in different places. It's not an exact science.

Wherever we come across these grey areas, we will flag them up and give you the tools to make informed judgements in your own writing and your own teaching. What we hope we'll do in the process is reassure you that the grammar pedants are deceiving you – there aren't massive lists of rules out there about grammar that you don't know. There are just conventions and most of them are completely familiar to you. In many of the cases where you think you 'don't know the rules' (e.g. *when do I use single inverted commas and when do I use double inverted commas?*), it's because there are a whole range of acceptable options and it's entirely down to your own preference.

The grammar curriculum

Before we get too misty-eyed about the boundless freedom to be enjoyed by taking a descriptive approach to grammar, we need a reality check. We've talked a lot about irritating grammar pedants making up rules and then trying to enforce them on other people. The bad news is that, at the time of writing, quite a few of them still work at the Department for Education and they're still producing a national test that all children in maintained schools in England have to sit at the end of Key Stage 1 and Key Stage 2. These tests are all about using 'correct' grammar, which sits awkwardly with what we've already told you. This is nothing to worry about and, as we make our way through the chapters of this book, we'll make sure that you understand everything you need to teach your pupils to ensure that they're ready.

One of the many valid criticisms one hears levelled at the current approach to grammar in the primary curriculum is that it feels somewhat divorced from the business of actually learning to write. We've provided examples of teaching ideas and resources you can use in each of the chapters but we also hope to equip you with the knowledge and confidence you'll need to teach grammar within the rest of the English curriculum – not as a separate inconvenience.

On page 197, we've included an edited and abridged version of the glossary of grammar terms from the primary National Curriculum with page references to where they are discussed in this book. If you need to find out about a particular topic, this will enable you to reach the information you need quickly and easily. We've also included a 'frequently asked questions' section on page 203. This will tell you where to find the solutions to some of the most common puzzles that primary school teachers find themselves wrestling with when trying to teach grammar.

We weren't taught much grammar at school in any formal sense and nor, in all likelihood, were you. This is one of the reasons why the grammar, punctuation and spelling aspect of the National Curriculum causes stress for teachers of primary English up and down the country. We have both been in the position of having to get our heads around grammatical concepts (subjunctive mood, anyone?) in order to teach them, and understand the anxiety that can cause. One aim of this book is to alleviate that anxiety. We wanted to write a book that would provide clear and simple explanations of the concepts and jargon you need to know, alongside practical ideas for teaching it to your pupils. In every chapter, you will find a simple, accessible breakdown of key ideas in English grammar, alongside a selection of activities and lesson ideas you can bring straight into your classroom to make grammar interesting and meaningful for young learners.

However, we want this book to do more than that. The truth is that, while there is so much about the current educational climate that concerns us, we do believe in teaching grammar and in giving it more attention than perhaps schools tended to in the past. If we ruled the world then one of the changes we would make (apart from making cheese a national dish) is that grammar teaching wouldn't be centred around a dull and somewhat arbitrary Year 6 test. It would involve looking creatively at the mechanics of how our language works, exploring patterns and giving children the linguistic tools to express themselves with flair and conviction. It's always easy to say of any educational experience that we never had ourselves, 'I never did that and it never did me any harm', which is pretty much where we started on this journey. Being honest with ourselves over the last few years, we've started to realise that this is a cop-out: an easy excuse to turn our backs on something that will require us to change our habits and challenge our own thinking. Instead, we have started to alter our habits and question our preconceptions about grammar.

Understanding how language is used and examining how we generate meaning when we speak and write is never a waste of time. It goes to the heart of human interaction and it tells the story of how our language and culture evolved. Learning about grammar is not a matter of memorising 'rules'. While there are of course certain conventions that we firmly encourage you to observe, our primary focus will be on describing how people use English grammar to convey meaning and influence their audience, be it a reader or a listener.

This book is for Ms Armstrong, Mr Yildiz, Mrs Patterson and everyone else who needs a bit of extra help with primary grammar. This is the book we wish we'd been given when we first had to teach the new grammar curriculum. We hope that it will take away your fear of grammar and give you the confidence to teach it well. We hope that it will be informative and give you the answers to all the specific questions you have. Perhaps most importantly, we hope that it will make you feel positive about grammar and see the value in teaching children about it.

How to use this book

This book is divided into 18 chapters arranged in three parts. We'd be delighted if you felt inclined to read the whole thing from cover to cover, but you're probably more likely to focus on particular topics that you're slightly confused about or struggling to teach. If you've opened up this book looking for the answer to a specific grammar question, we suggest you take a look at the 'frequently asked questions' on page 203. A lot of the grammar confusion that causes teachers unspoken embarrassment is more common than they think.

What will I find in each part?

Part One of the book is called **Making sense**. It introduces the basic building blocks of sentence construction and most of the word classes or parts of speech. It explores the ideas of subject and object and it tackles common misconceptions about apostrophes and plurals. There may be a temptation to skip or brush over the details in this section, especially if you are teaching older children. However, the contents of Part One are the fundamental building blocks of English grammar; without a secure understanding of all these concepts, children may struggle to grasp the more abstract ideas introduced later on.

    Part Two is called **Extending sentences**. As you'd imagine from the title, it deals with the wide variety of ways in which children can move beyond simple and obvious sentence structures in their writing, employing a wider range of techniques to get their ideas across with precision. It explores the different types of clause and phrase, offering clarity on the differences between them, which is often lacking in online reference resources. It also addresses the questions you've always been too afraid to ask about commas and semi-colons, speech punctuation, quotation marks and parenthesis.

    Part Three is called **Writing with flair** and this is really about moving from proficiency to mastery. It deals with the functions of sentences and the way in which subtle changes in word order can alter the effect on the reader. It explores the different grammatical 'moods' and the challenges of incorporating these into one's writing effectively. It concludes with Chapter 18: Breaking the 'rules'. Here we explore the ways in which one can defy the usual conventions of grammar to enhance the effect of one's writing. We will tackle puns, poetry, one-word sentences and much more.

    At the end of the book, you will find seven **appendices** providing a bit of extra background to some of the conventions we have discussed. They are designed to help you, as teacher, to understand the grammar curriculum in greater depth. The content of these sections goes beyond what children need to understand by the end of Year 6, but you may find they will provide you with an additional level of knowledge that enables you to answer some of those trickier questions that pupils have a habit of throwing at you in Years 5 and 6. While there is no statutory requirement to teach the content in the appendices, you may find it useful to do so in certain instances.

What will I find in each chapter?

Each chapter starts with **What you need to know**, which explains everything you need to understand in order to teach that particular topic confidently. The second half of each chapter offers a variety of **Teaching ideas** for delivering this content to your class. The best thing you can do for your class is to understand the concepts really thoroughly yourself, explain them clearly to your pupils and then give them plenty of opportunities to practise using and applying their knowledge of grammar. Nonetheless, you may find some of the teaching ideas in each chapter a useful accompaniment to this. Next to each teaching idea, you will see a logo that tells you whether it is suitable for:

KS1 Key Stage 1: Years 1 and 2.

LKS2 Lower Key Stage 2: Years 3 and 4.

UKS2 Upper Key Stage 2: Years 5 and 6.

When you see this logo 🖱, it means that accompanying resources are available to download from www.bloomsbury.com/the-grammar-book. These include modelled texts, worksheets, templates and much more.

In each chapter overview, we have highlighted the sections that are relevant to Key Stage 1 (KS1), lower Key Stage 2 (LKS2) and upper Key Stage 2 (UKS2). You'll find most of what you need to cover in Key Stage 1 in Part One (with a few exceptions such as commas). If you are a Key Stage 2 teacher, then everything you need to cover with your class is in Parts One to Three.

Most of the information you will find in this book is available elsewhere but, as teachers, we have always been frustrated with the way in which it tends to be presented and organised. We've thought carefully about the progression in this book and how and when you should introduce each concept. This is a book by teachers for teachers and we hope that it will give you the sort of clarity and honesty you need.

A final thought before you dive in

We want to equip you to discharge your statutory duties and teach your pupils what they need to know to excel in the grammar, punctuation and spelling tests in Years 2 and 6. Far more importantly, however, we want to equip you to explore the weird and wonderful grey areas of grammar – to celebrate the inconsistencies and debate the uncertainties. We want you to use an enhanced understanding of grammar to celebrate the English language with your pupils so that they can take it and make it sing.

What you need to cover

With all the changes that have happened over the last few years, it is unsurprising that the first question lots of teachers have is '*What* grammar do I need to teach my class?' Every school seems to have its own scheme of work and its own way of doing things. The content you are statutorily required to teach is outlined on the Department for Education website. However, for those who don't have the time to trawl through dozens of documents, here is the content you are required to cover in each year group, from Year 1 to Year 6. You can use the table to help you find the chapters in this book that are most relevant to your current year group. The Department for Education (2013a) is keen to stress that this table shows 'when concepts should be introduced, not necessarily when they should be completely understood'. These concepts should be revisited repeatedly to consolidate them.

Key Stage 1		
Year 1		**Chapter(s)**
Word	• Regular plural noun suffixes -s or -es (for example, *dog*, *dogs*; *wish*, *wishes*) and the effects of these suffixes on the meaning of the noun. • Suffixes that can be added to verbs where no change is needed in the spelling of root words (e.g. *helping*, *helped*, *helper*).	1 and 4
Sentence	• How words can combine to make sentences. • Joining words and clauses using *and*.	5 and 11
Text	• Sequencing sentences to form short narratives.	17
Punctuation	• Introduction to capital letters, full stops, question marks and exclamation marks to demarcate sentences. • Capital letters for names and for the personal pronoun *I*.	8 and 2
Year 2		
Word	• Formation of nouns using suffixes such as -ness, -er and by compounding (for example, *whiteboard*, *superman*). • Formation of adjectives using suffixes such as -ful, -less. • Use of the suffixes -er, -est in adjectives and the use of -ly to turn adjectives into adverbs.	1 and 6

Sentence	<ul><li>Subordinating conjunctions (*when*, *if*, *that*, *because*).</li><li>Coordinating conjunctions (*or*, *and*, *but*).</li><li>Expanded noun phrases for description and specification (for example, *the blue butterfly*, *plain flour*, *the man in the moon*).</li><li>Identifying the purpose of sentences as statements, questions, exclamations or commands.</li></ul>	11, 12 and 16
Text	<ul><li>Correct choice and consistent use of present tense and past tense throughout writing.</li><li>Use of the progressive form of verbs in the present tense and past tense to mark actions in progress (for example, *she is drumming*, *he was shouting*).</li></ul>	4
Punctuation	<ul><li>Use of capital letters, full stops, question marks and exclamation marks to demarcate sentences.</li><li>Commas to separate items in a list.</li><li>Apostrophes to mark where letters are missing in spelling and to mark singular possession in nouns (for example, *the girl's name*).</li></ul>	8, 13 and 7

Key Stage 2		
Year 3		Chapter(s)
Word	<ul><li>Formation of nouns using a range of prefixes (for example, *super-*, *anti-*, *auto-*).</li><li>Use of the forms *a* or *an* according to whether the next word begins with a consonant or a vowel (for example, *a rock*, *an open box*).</li></ul>	1 and 3
Sentence	<ul><li>Expressing time, place and cause using conjunctions (for example, *when*, *before*, *after*, *while*, *so*, *because*), adverbs (for example, *then*, *next*, *soon*, *therefore*), or prepositions (for example, *before*, *after*, *during*, *in*, *because of*).</li></ul>	11 and 6
Text	<ul><li>Introduction to paragraphs as a way to group related material.</li><li>Use of the present perfect form of verbs instead of the simple past (for example, *He has gone out to play* contrasted with *He went out to play*).</li></ul>	17 and 4
Punctuation	<ul><li>Introduction to inverted commas to punctuate direct speech.</li></ul>	15
Year 4		
Word	<ul><li>The grammatical difference between plural and possessive -s.</li></ul>	7
Sentence	<ul><li>Noun phrases expanded by the addition of modifying adjectives, nouns and prepositional phrases (e.g. *the teacher* expanded to *the strict maths teacher with curly hair*).</li><li>Fronted adverbials (e.g. *later that day*, *we went to the cinema*).</li></ul>	12 and 6
Text	<ul><li>Use of paragraphs to organise ideas around a theme.</li><li>Appropriate choice of pronoun or noun within and across sentences to aid cohesion and avoid repetition.</li></ul>	17

Punctuation	• Use of inverted commas and other punctuation to indicate direct speech (for example, a comma after the reporting clause; end punctuation within inverted commas: *The conductor shouted, 'Sit down!'*). • Apostrophes to mark plural possession (for example, *the girl's name*, *the girls' names*). • Use of commas after fronted adverbials (e.g. *after they had finished eating, they cleared the table*).	15, 7 and 13
Year 5		
Word	• Converting nouns or adjectives into verbs using suffixes (for example, -ate, -ise, -ify). • Verb prefixes (for example, dis-, de-, mis-, over- and re-).	18 and 1
Sentence	• Relative clauses beginning with *who, which, where, when, whose, that*, or an omitted relative pronoun. • Indicating degrees of possibility using adverbs (for example, *perhaps, surely*) or modal verbs (for example, *might, should, will, must*).	10, 6 and 4
Text	• Devices to build cohesion within a paragraph (for example, *then, after that, this, firstly*). • Linking ideas across paragraphs using adverbials of time (for example, *later*), place (for example, *nearby*) and number (for example, *secondly*) or tense choices (for example, *he had seen her before*).	17
Punctuation	• Brackets, dashes or commas to indicate parenthesis. • Use of commas to clarify meaning or avoid ambiguity.	14 and 13
Year 6		
Word	• The difference between vocabulary typical of informal speech and vocabulary appropriate for formal speech and writing (for example, *find out – discover; ask for – request; go in – enter*).	17
Sentence	• Use of the passive to affect the presentation of information in a sentence (for example, *Tom broke the window in the greenhouse* versus *The window in the greenhouse was broken by Tom)*. • The difference between structures typical of informal speech and structures appropriate for formal speech and writing (for example, the use of question tags: *He's your friend, isn't he?*). • The use of subjunctive forms such as *If I were* or *Were they to come* in some very formal writing and speech.	16 and 17
Text	• Linking ideas across paragraphs using a wider range of cohesive devices: repetition of a word or phrase, grammatical connections (for example, the use of adverbials such as *on the other hand, in contrast*, or *as a consequence*), and ellipsis. • Layout devices to structure a text (for example, headings, sub-headings and bullet points).	17

| Punctuation | • Use of the semi-colon, colon and dash to mark the boundary between independent clauses (for example, *It's raining; I'm fed up*).
• Use of the colon to introduce a list and use of semi-colons within lists.
• Punctuation of bullet points to list information.
• How hyphens can be used to avoid ambiguity (for example, *man eating shark* versus *man-eating shark*, or *recover* versus *re-cover*). | 14, 17 and 1 |

Adapted from Department for Education (2013a).

Part One

Making sense

Chapter 1
Writing words

Chapter overview

Let's start at the very beginning. In this chapter we will be looking at how we put sounds together to create meaning. Or, in technical terms:

• How phonemes, graphemes, digraphs and trigraphs are combined to make words.	KS1	Pages 16–17
• How compound words can be divided into their root words, prefixes and suffixes.	KS1 LKS2	Pages 17–18
• When and how to use hyphens.	LKS2 UKS2	Pages 18–19
• Ideas and resources to support teaching of these concepts.	KS1 LKS2 UKS2	Pages 19–22

Most of this book is about how whole words are arranged to create and modify meaning. However, before we dive into all that, it's worth taking some time to look at words themselves, specifically how they're made and how they can change in different circumstances. This is not primarily a book about spelling, but spelling and grammar cannot be disconnected entirely. So, let's start at the very beginning – with the very building blocks of our language.

What you need to know

Your relationship with grammar began before your earliest memories were formed. From the moment we discover that we can combine sounds to modify their effects on another person, we are dealing with grammar. There is probably something we could call grammar in a baby's cries. English grammar begins when we first start to make sounds within the context of the English language. So, we need to start our journey at the same place that English teaching in primary schools often begins: with phonics. Some of the information in this section will be second nature to Early Years specialists but, if you've spent most of your career in Key Stage 2, it's important to make yourself aware of these basic ideas.

Letters and sounds: phonemes, graphemes, digraphs and trigraphs

As most children in Early Years can tell you, there are 26 letters in the English alphabet: five vowels and 21 consonants. The vowels (*a*, *e*, *i*, *o* and *u*) correspond roughly to the sounds, also known as phonemes, that we can make by allowing air to flow freely out of our throats and mouths. The consonant sounds made by all the other letters of the alphabet require us to use our teeth, tongue, lips or palate to alter the sound of air escaping from our throats and mouths. That said, the letter *y* corresponds to vowel sounds in some words, such as *tiny* or *rhythm*. While there are usually one or more specific sounds that we associate with each letter, we can also generate completely different phonemes using combinations of different letter sounds. The written representation of a phoneme, whether it's composed of one letter or a combination of letters, is known as a grapheme.

When these graphemes are formed of two letters, we call them digraphs, for example the grapheme made by the letters *ph* in *phone* or by the letters *ea* in *read*. Sometimes, a digraph is formed of two vowels split by a consonant. For example, by adding the letter *e* to the word *hat*, it becomes *hate*, changing the sound of the *a*. When we were at school, this was taught as 'magic e'. Partly to sound more intellectual, and partly to sound less like they've misspent their summers in the nightclubs of the Balearic Islands, teachers nowadays are encouraged to use the more technical name: a split digraph. Some graphemes are formed of three letters, such as the letters *tch* in *match* or the letters *igh* in *high*, and these are known as trigraphs.

The representation of specific sounds by specific letters or groups of letters is not consistent in English. In fact, the most common sound in the English spoken language is the unstressed vowel sound known as a schwa (which is quite fun to say – SCHWA!). A schwa can be found represented on the page by any of the five vowels:

Cellar

Brother

Nastily

London

Saturday

When the words above are read aloud, each of the underlined vowels sounds exactly the same. This is one reason why learning to spell in English is so tricky and it also explains why our language contains so many homophones: words with two different spellings (and meanings) with exactly the same pronunciation, such as *lesson* and *lessen* or *stationary* and *stationery*.

Combining letters and sounds according to the capricious conventions of the English language gives us words. Words have differing numbers of <u>syllables</u> – units of speech usually centred around an individual vowel sound:

Dog	*Dog*	one syllable
Chaos	*Cha* | *os*	two syllables
Damaging	*Dam* | *ag* | *ing*	three syllables
Apostrophe	*Ap* | *os* | *tro* | *phe*	four syllables

Morphemes: root words, prefixes and suffixes, and compound words

So far, we've established how letters can be used to create sounds but we still haven't got to the point where these sounds start to have meaning. At what point does that change? Like the moment in our evolutionary history when amino acids formed into proteins and life was breathed into the first ever organisms, there is a magical point where graphemes and phonemes, and the words and syllables they generate, become more than mere squiggles and grunts. There is a point when they start to *mean* something – that is where the story of English grammar begins and that is where we start our own journey into the art of making sense.

The very smallest unit of meaning in our language is a <u>morpheme</u>, and no, sadly, this isn't a narcotic for calming the nerves of primary school teachers. Consider this word:

Cat

Those three squiggles refer to something else. When you see them, you cannot help but imagine a four-legged mammal with pointy ears and whiskers. That reference requires the presence of these three letters, nothing more and nothing less. This word, therefore, is a morpheme: a single unit of meaning with a single reference. Now consider this word:

Unhelpful

This word is rather more complicated and its meaning is formed from three parts, or morphemes: a <u>prefix</u>, a <u>root word</u> and a <u>suffix</u>:

Un | help | ful

Just as the roots of a tree form the basis for its trunk, the root of a word forms the basis for its meaning. A prefix is a separate morpheme that comes *before* the root word and a suffix is a separate morpheme that comes *after* the root word. In this case, the root word is *help-*, which refers to the concept of offering assistance to someone else. This is followed by the suffix *-ful*, one of many suffixes in English that turn a noun into an adjective (more on this in Chapter 18: Breaking the 'rules', page 171), so that the word (*helpful*) now refers to the quality of being keen to offer assistance to someone else. The root word is also preceded by the prefix **un-**, one of several prefixes that *negates*, or reverses, the meaning of the word following it. Other prefixes that do this include *de-*, *non-*, *in-*, *im-*, *ex-*, *anti-*, *dis-*, *mis-* and *a-*. After the negating prefix has been added, the word now refers to the quality of being unwilling to offer assistance to someone else.

Prefixes and suffixes can have all sorts of meanings. As well as providing negations, for example, some prefixes indicate how many of something there are or how widespread it is (*mono-*, *multi-*, *tri-*, *uni-*, *pan-*), some indicate when or where something happens or takes place (*pre-*, *post-*, *inter-*, *extra-*, *out-*) and some deal with size or scale (*mini-*, *micro-*, *mega-*, *super-*, *hyper-*). As well as determining the <u>word class</u> of a root word (whether it is a noun, verb, adjective, etc. – see later chapters for more on all of these), suffixes can determine <u>verb tense</u> (*-en*, *-ed*, *-ing*) or indicate <u>plurals</u> (*-s*, *-es*, *-es*, *-ves*).

Sometimes, two root words can be combined to make a <u>compound word</u>. Compounding is a posh grammatical term for putting two things together – usually two things of equal importance. A compound word is a single word composed of two or more root words, for example:

Shopkeeper

Backdate

Butterfly

Makeover

Bittersweet

Hyphens

Sometimes, two words can be joined by a <u>hyphen</u> (-) so that they stand as a single word.

People get themselves worked up over hyphens, worrying about specific rules that don't exist. The vast majority of these rules are entirely optional and, interestingly, the use of hyphens is declining across the English-speaking world. Worrying about imaginary rules is a common theme of this book and, as we explore the conventions of grammar, you may find that there are several instances where you've been worrying needlessly. So let's look at some cases where you would usually use hyphens and some where it really doesn't matter.

One instance where hyphens really do make your meaning clearer are what we call <u>compound modifiers</u>: two words used to describe something, often adjectives or adverbs or the participle form of a verb. (The later chapters in this section explain more about these word classes.)

Is he a self-made man or is he from a long-established family?

Without the hyphen, this sentence would be a lot more confusing, so, in instances like this, we probably want the hyphen to stay. Often, the question you should ask yourself when making decisions about grammar is not 'Am I obeying the rules?' but 'Does this make sense?' In the sentence above, for example, the hyphen between *long* and *established* makes it absolutely clear that the writer is enquiring as to whether *the family is long-established*, as opposed to whether the *established family is long*. 'Good grammar' is often that which eliminates confusion or ambiguity. This often applies to <u>compound nouns</u> too:

I bought a Jack-in-the-box for my three-year-old.

In the sentence above, two individual nouns have each been made out of several separate words. The hyphen makes it much easier to read, immediately signalling to the reader that, in each case, the three hyphenated words are intended to be understood as a single entity.

There are several other instances in which you might see hyphens being used. They are often used after prefixes that end with the same letter as the root word they precede, e.g. *co-ordinate* or *re-energise*, to avoid potential confusion at the sight of a double vowel. These hyphens are completely optional. They're also used when a prefix or suffix is being added to a root word to create a phrase that may be new or unfamiliar to the reader, e.g. *ex-army* or *post-9/11*. Hyphens can also separate two parts of a word when you run out of space at the end of a line. Some teachers discourage this, preferring that their pupils check that they have enough space for the word before they put pen to paper but, again, this is entirely up to you.

It's impossible to list all the stylistic uses of hyphens that you might come across. You'll often see them used in direct speech between every letter of a word to indicate that a character is spelling it out, or between the individual syllables of the word to indicate that the pronunciation is unfamiliar to the character. The long and the short of it is that hyphens are used to separate parts of a word and you use them when it will aid your reader to do so.

Hyphens are not to be confused with *en dashes* (see Chapter 14, page 138), even though they look almost identical. While a hyphen separates parts of a single word or compound word, dashes separate entire phrases or clauses within a sentence.

Teaching ideas

The following ideas are suitable for teaching root words, prefixes and suffixes, compound words and hyphens to Key Stage 1 and Key Stage 2 pupils.

The suffixes -ful and -less

`KS1`

When introducing your pupils to suffixes, start by explaining what the suffix means, for example:

- ful means 'full of'
- less means 'without'.

Your pupils can practise adding these suffixes and using the new words in a sentence by completing the following table. There is a worksheet to support this activity online.

+ful	Root word	+less
Careful		*Careless*
You have to be careful when crossing the road.	Care	*He was careless and knocked over the vase.*
	Hope	
	Fear	
	Doubt	
	Help	
	Power	
	Joy	

KS1
LKS2
UKS2

Compound word match-up

Split these 15 compound words into the root words and write them onto 30 sticky labels. For example, 'breakfast' would be written on two labels: 'break' and 'fast'.

Breakfast

Goalkeeper

Paintbrush

Butterfly

Goldfish

Sandpaper

Lipstick

Sunflower

Cupcake

Caretaker

Bookshelf

Raincoat

Football

Moonlight

Fishmonger

Stick one label on each pupil in your class and challenge them to find their partner to make a compound word. Once all the pupils have found their partner, get them to swap labels and repeat the activity.

Root word challenge

LKS2

UKS2

This is an activity that you can introduce once your class have a secure understanding of what a root word is and can use a range of prefixes and suffixes accurately. To start with, give your pupils a root word, e.g.:

Act

Challenge your pupils to add prefixes and suffixes to create as many words as they can with the root word, e.g.:

Action

Acting

Actor

React

Acted

Activate

Active

Actively

Deactivate

Crazy compound words

LKS2

UKS2

This is a sequence of activities to consolidate children's understanding of compound words. The first task requires pupils to match pictures that create compound words, for example 'book' and 'shelf' make 'bookshelf'. The second task is about identifying compound words in a sentence and matching words together to create compound words. The resource is available at: http://resources.hwb.wales.gov.uk/VTC/crazy_comp_words/eng/Introduction/default.htm.

Hyphen hunt

UKS2

Pupils use the following list of words to generate compound adjectives and write them out with the hyphen. There are multiple solutions to this activity and a worksheet is provided in the online resources to help you facilitate it.

Fire	Lit	Minded	Liked	Breathing
Ill	Eyed	Deep	Pocketed	Open
Blooded	Baked	Disposed	Hearted	Willed
Fitting	Warm	Well	Cold	Half
Well	Strong	Kindly	Green	

Chapter 2

Types of noun

Chapter overview

If you've ever wondered why the Queen is a proper noun but a queen is common, then you are in the right place. In this chapter we will look at:

• The distinction between proper and common nouns.	**KS1**	Pages 24–25
• The distinction between concrete and abstract nouns.	**LKS2**	Pages 25–26
• The distinction between countable and uncountable nouns.	**LKS2**	Pages 26–27
• How to use collective nouns.	**LKS2**	Pages 27–28
• Ideas and resources to support teaching of these concepts.	**KS1** **LKS2** **LKS2**	Pages 28–32

This is a topic that teachers think they understand inside out but it contains more metaphorical banana skins than you might think!

If you're currently a Key Stage 1 teacher, you may want to turn straight to the section on concrete nouns, as this is an excellent starting point for younger children. If you are currently teaching any year group in Key Stage 2, then there is information you may want to share with your class in the whole of this chapter. If you're here to find out more about noun phrases, then please turn to Chapter 12, page 119.

What you need to know

You're a noun and so am I. All of your friends and relatives, all the towns and countries you've ever visited, all your possessions and all of the thoughts, feelings and ideas that have ever passed through your head are nouns.

Nouns are things. They are the stuff our sentences are about. *Table*, *otter*, *event*, *President Obama*, *loneliness* and *Christmas* are all usually nouns, e.g.:

We have bought a new kitchen <u>table</u>.
<u>Christmas</u> is on the 25th of December.
Older people sometimes struggle with <u>loneliness</u>.

A word can change word class depending on how it's used. The word *time*, for example, can be either a noun or a verb.

In this sentence, *time* is a concept; it is the thing that is flying. Therefore it is a noun:

<u>Time</u> flies when you're having fun.

In this sentence, *time* tells you how the boy (a noun) is being asked to act, so it is a verb:

The girl asked the boy to <u>time</u> her while she ran 100 metres.

There are different ways of classifying nouns. A noun is *either* proper or common, it is *either* abstract or concrete, and it is *either* countable or uncountable. When you're teaching children about nouns, it's likely you'll want to start with proper and common nouns, so we'll begin there too.

Proper or common

Proper nouns are names of specific things. They could, for example, be the names of people, places, festivals or months of the year: *The Beatles*, *London*, *Ramadan* and *Charlotte* are usually proper nouns. Proper nouns begin with a capital letter, e.g.:

<u>Rajni</u> lives in <u>Manchester</u>.

When a proper noun is made up of two words, both words would start with a capital letter, e.g.:

<u>Queen Victoria</u> was married to <u>Prince Albert</u>.

Unlike proper nouns, common nouns are the names of non-specific things, e.g. *cat*, *pencils*, *bravery*, *festival* and *cheese*. So, whereas *London* is usually a proper noun because it refers to one specific named place, the word *city* is usually a common noun because it refers to the idea of a city generally:

It's always exciting to visit a new <u>city</u>.

A common noun does not usually start with a capital letter unless it begins a sentence or forms part of a title.

As we said in the introduction, language doesn't always behave according to our so-called rules, and whether a noun is proper or common is sometimes debatable. Consider these two sentences:

My favourite subjects are English and maths.
My favourite subjects are English and Maths.

This is a common dilemma for primary school teachers. We always capitalise *English* because it is the name of a specific language as well as a subject at school. However, what should we do with *maths*? Which of these sentences is correct? In fact, neither of these sentences is more or less 'correct' than the other. Whether or not mathematics and maths are treated as proper nouns is up for grabs – so don't worry and do whatever feels right for you!

Concrete or abstract

Concrete nouns refer to things that have a specific size and/or location. They are often children's first words because they refer to things that they can see or things that they can reach out and touch, e.g. *sand*, *Mum*, *Scotland* and *egg* would usually be concrete nouns:

<u>Scotland</u> is to the north of England.
I have got <u>sand</u> in my shoes.

Abstract nouns refer to things without a specific size or location. These are often, although not always, emotions and ideas that exist in the mind, e.g. *betrayal*, *honour*, *compassion* and *guilt* are usually abstract nouns. These examples are the sort of abstract noun we often think of when we're teaching children; however, any concepts without a specific size or location are usually abstract nouns, for example: *question*, *probability*, *Hinduism*, *Christmas*, *athletics*, *challenge*.

<u>Athletics</u> was an important part of Ancient Greek culture.
I wish it could be <u>Christmas</u> every day.

Some nouns can be abstract or concrete depending on how they're used. Think about these two sentences:

Yusuf likes <u>football</u>.
Yusuf bought a new <u>football</u>.

In the first of these sentences, *football* refers to a game played in all sorts of places by all sorts of people all over the world. It has no specific size or location and therefore it is an abstract noun. In the second sentence, the word *football* refers to a specific object Yusuf has bought that has a specific size and a specific location, so it is a concrete noun.

And, once again, there are situations where it is debatable whether a noun is abstract or concrete. Consider this sentence:

I think my <u>mind</u> is playing tricks on me.

If you interpret the word *mind* in this sentence to mean exactly the same as *brain*, then you are using it as a concrete noun because it refers to a specific object with a specific size and location. However, if you interpret it to mean a complicated mixture of thoughts and instincts without a specific size or location, then you are using it as an abstract noun. Neither of these interpretations is any more or less 'right' than the other. Once again, it is worth emphasising that these distinctions are not 'rules' and the way we use language doesn't always fit into neat little boxes.

Countable or uncountable

Countable nouns, as the name suggests, are things we can count: *sofas, children, suggestions* or *animals* are usually countable nouns:

We have two <u>sofas</u>.
Craig has three <u>children</u>.
I'd like to make several <u>suggestions</u>.

Uncountable nouns, as you'd imagine, are nouns we don't count, e.g. *rubbish, equipment* and *weather* are often uncountable nouns. Notice that any attempt to count these nouns would look wrong:

~~**There are at least eight <u>rubbishes</u> in that bin.**~~

As always, whether a noun is countable or uncountable is not fixed and depends entirely on the context of the sentence. For example:

There are six <u>spaces</u> in the car park.
There is not enough <u>space</u> in the car park.

In the first sentence, there are a specific number of spaces; therefore *space* is a countable noun. The second sentence refers to all the space in the car park, regardless of how it has been divided into individual units.

Is it fewer or less?

Those insufferably smug grammar pedants we met in the introduction often can't help chipping in with something like, 'I think you mean you have *fewer* pupils in today, not *less*.' This is something people have a tendency to take far more seriously than perhaps they need to. However, it is something you will have to teach Key Stage 2 children and it's a question that a lot of adults seek clarification about.

Whether you use *fewer* or *less* is all to do with uncountable and countable nouns. When quantifying **countable** nouns we use *fewer* and when quantifying **uncountable** nouns we use *less*. Have a look at these examples:

The <u>fewer crimes</u> you commit, the <u>less trouble</u> you will find yourself in.

In this sentence, *crimes* is a countable noun and *trouble* is uncountable.

We may have <u>fewer soldiers</u>, but the opposing army has <u>less spirit</u>.

In this sentence, *soldiers* is a countable noun and *spirit* is uncountable.

While we're here, it's probably worth pointing out that the distinction between *much* and *many* is largely the same and it won't just be those grammar pedants who notice if you get this 'wrong'. It's also an error commonly made by young children, so it is worth teaching in Key Stage 1 if you have children who are struggling with it.

There <u>is too much water</u> and there <u>are too many ice cubes</u> in that glass.

In this sentence, *water* is preceded by *much* because it is uncountable, whereas *ice cubes* is preceded by *many* because it is countable. Some children, especially those with English as an additional language, might be inclined to use 'much' in both instances. This will make them stand out far more obviously than confusing *less* and *fewer* will and, for that reason, it is probably a good idea to correct them straightaway.

Collective nouns

Collective nouns describe a group of that thing, e.g.:

A <u>flock</u> of sheep.
A <u>group</u> of children.

We have a bit of an issue with collective nouns – not so much the fact of them but the way they are often taught to primary school children. For example, the fact that most children seem to be taught about a *murder* of crows before they can find Germany on a map seems a bit of an odd priority. It probably happens because we think the easiest way to teach children about collective nouns is to talk about different groups of animals. It makes sense: children like animals and lots of the books and films aimed at them will be about animals. Plus, once you've introduced a child to terms like '*a flock of sheep*' or '*a herd of cows*', it's not long until they're pestering you for the collective nouns for everything: crows, owls, dragons, etc.

However, there are more obvious collective nouns you could start with in Early Years and Key Stage 1. *Group, set* and *pile*, for example, are collective nouns that children are more likely to encounter than *herd, flock* or *parliament*. Indeed, it may be more useful for children to reflect on the subtle difference in meaning between *a pile of papers, a stack of papers* and *a heap of papers* than to identify the 'correct' collective noun for jellyfish (*fluther* or *smuck* if you're interested!).

Although they are often used to refer to several items (or something uncountable), collective nouns themselves are usually singular:

I'm looking through this <u>pile</u> of paper.
I saw a <u>gaggle</u> of geese.

Teaching ideas

Key Stage 1 children should have repeated exposure to the different types of noun, with clear explanations of how they are used. With Key Stage 2 children, you will probably want to explore the distinctions between different types of noun in more detail and how they impact on the other grammatical features of the sentence.

KS1 Clap when you hear...

Read a story to the class (or use the modelled text on page 31) and ask the children to clap when they hear a noun. You might want to extend this activity so that they clap a different number of times for different types of noun. Alternatively, ask a child to explain why they clapped and what type of noun they think they heard, e.g. *'Jack, you clapped during that sentence. What noun did you hear? Do you know what sort of noun that is?'*

KS1 Sing the noun song

Singing is often a good way to reinforce words and ideas in one's memory, and younger children tend to respond very well to it. So get online and find a noun song – there are dozens out there but the one we normally use is by Grammaropolis: www.youtube.com/watch?v=8kcJzh6gqGM. Although it may be mildly irritating to the adult ear, the children love it and you will be singing along after a few plays. Your class may even feel inspired to write their own song!

KS1 Paint a noun

Trying to draw or paint them is a great way to draw out the differences between the various types of noun. This could be particularly interesting when it comes to the distinction between abstract and concrete nouns. For example, during a lesson when children are painting or drawing a concrete object, e.g. life drawing of plants or fruit, discuss how we could create art to portray more abstract nouns such as sadness, courage or hope. You might show children pieces of art where the painter or sculptor has tried to convey an abstract noun such as fear (*The Scream* by Edvard Munch would be a good place to start) and explore the relationship between the concrete nouns depicted (the *man* on the *bridge*) and the abstract nouns they evoke. This will help children to connect the sense in which we use the word 'abstract' in grammar with the word's better-known application in art.

We're going on a noun hunt!

`KS1` `LKS2` `UKS2`

Once you've introduced your class to the different types of noun and you're happy they are secure with that knowledge, why not take your class around the school and its grounds to 'hunt' for nouns? They will no doubt be able to find plenty of concrete, common, countable nouns, such as *chairs*, *doors* and *children*. However, you might also want to encourage them to think more broadly about abstract and uncountable nouns: you could, for example, point out that in some corridors there is more *noise* whereas in others there is *silence*. Perhaps they can find children putting *effort* into their work or two people having a *conversation*. This activity can be extended or simplified in any number of ways, making it just as suitable for Year 6 (who might be asked to identify that 'effort' was visible in a particular classroom) as for Year 1 (who might simply want to identify that 'chairs' are present!).

Colour them in!

`KS1` `LKS2` `UKS2`

Give the children an age-appropriate text (or use the modelled examples on page 31). Read the text as a class, introducing the new vocabulary as you go. Then challenge your pupils to identify the different types of noun. You could create a key as a class, e.g. colour all common nouns in blue, proper nouns in red, etc. Children could complete this activity independently or in pairs.

Science nouns

`KS1` `LKS2` `UKS2`

Perhaps more than any other subject, science is full of nouns that could be considered abstract or concrete depending on your point of view. Consider the words *gravity*, *force* and *Newtons* in the sentence, *'The Earth's gravity exerts a force of 9.83 Newtons.'* Are these abstract or concrete nouns? You can argue the toss to different extents for each of them – and doing so will be a good way to help pupils to explore their understanding of all three concepts. This is equally true of many other scientific words: *electricity*, *light*, *sound*, *offspring*, etc.

Noun debate

`LKS2` `UKS2`

We shouldn't be afraid of teaching the grey areas of grammar and what better way to do it than encouraging children to debate contestable issues? As you teach children about nouns, you will come across 'grey areas': situations where a noun is neither clearly one type nor the other. For example, in the sentence, *'I opened my eyes and I was greeted by a wondrous sight'*, is *sight* an abstract or a concrete noun?

It's worth taking the time to discuss and debate which classifications are most suitable in such situations. This could be done in pairs or as a whole class. You should ensure that you encourage children to give good reasons for their opinions, rather than reaching a single 'correct answer'.

Venn diagram nouns

`LKS2` `UKS2`

Ask your pupils to draw three overlapping circles, labelling one 'common', another 'concrete' and the third 'countable'. Ask them to find a selection of nouns (once again, you might want to use the modelled writing on page 31 of this chapter to generate them) and place them in the appropriate places on the Venn diagram. Discuss how some nouns fall into more than one category depending on the context.

Noun substitution

Using the modelled example on page 31, ask pupils to find a replacement for each noun by finding an appropriate synonym, e.g.:
This sentence:

Alice felt anxiety rising within her <u>gut</u> as she looked at the strange collection of signs.

Could become:

Alice felt anxiety rising within her <u>stomach</u> as she looked at the strange collection of signs.

In addition to reinforcing their understanding of the different types of noun, this activity will help to develop your pupils' vocabulary as they search for a different word. This could lead to a discussion about how some synonyms are more relevant than others. In the aforementioned example, a pupil using a thesaurus might have found the word 'colon' as a synonym for gut! Take the opportunity to discuss how this would change the tone of the sentence.

Abstract nouns in maths

Many children who find maths difficult can find it challenging to picture or conceptualise the scenarios described in worded problems. You may sometimes find that it helps to identify the types of noun they can see. Consider the following problem:

> 'Bob is 1.36m tall and Charlotte is 1.27m tall. What is the difference between Bob's height and Charlotte's height?'

If you ask a child to identify the abstract nouns in the problem, they will pick out the word 'difference' and two instances of the word 'height'. If they are then able to explain how each of these words is being used in the sentence, they will be pretty close to solving the problem.

Much of primary maths is about the relationship between the abstract and the concrete. For example, understanding that halves, quarters, sevenths and tenths can be abstract or concrete nouns depending on the context is an essential, though usually unspoken, step in understanding fractions.

Maths is also a useful context in which to have noun debates (as described on page 29). Is *whole* an abstract or a concrete noun? What about *zero* or *infinity*? Questions like these will challenge children to combine their understanding of maths and English in a demanding way.

Abstract or concrete

In RE, a subject about specific named ideas and traditions, children will meet a lot of nouns of an unusual sort: those that are proper, abstract and uncountable. The names of religions and belief systems themselves (*Christianity, Islam, Judaism, Hinduism, Humanism,* etc.) are usually used in this way, as well as many of their festivals and rituals: *Christmas, Eucharist, Haj, Chanukah,* etc. The same is arguably true of the word *'God'* itself, which could lend itself to the mother of all 'noun debates' if you're brave enough to go down that path!

Modelled texts

The following modelled texts can be used in several of the previous teaching ideas. There are downloadable versions of both texts in the online resources, so you can print them, display them on a whiteboard or integrate them into worksheets.

Key Stage 1

One day, Dylan the Dinosaur had an idea. A thought popped into his head while he sat on the grass and looked up at the Moon.

'Maybe I could build a rocket and go on a journey to the Moon,' Dylan said.

Dylan went into the shed at the back of his garden and looked for the set of tools he got for Christmas. He also found a heap of old rusty metal, which he poured into a bucket. After that, he walked down the road to the house of his friend, Myrtle the Mammoth. He walked up the flight of steps that led to her door and rang the bell.

'Hi Dylan,' Myrtle said. 'What are you doing standing on my doorstep with all those tools and all that metal?'

'I want to build a rocket and go on a journey to the Moon,' Dylan said, 'but I need you to give me some help.'

'The Moon is made of cheese,' replied Myrtle, swinging her trunk thoughtfully. 'I don't really like cheese. I'm not sure this trip is really my cup of tea.'

Key Stage 2

Alice felt anxiety rising within her gut as she looked at the strange collection of signs. 'They're all in Latin!' she exclaimed.

'This is Ancient Rome!' Aurelius replied. 'Latin is the only language most of these people can understand.'

Time travel, it seemed, entailed challenges that Alice hadn't thought about.

'We'll have to do something about those clothes as well,' Aurelius said to her. 'You can't go and meet great figures from history wearing jeans and a t-shirt!'

A wave of dizziness swept over Alice as she watched the crowds of people all walking in the same direction with a real sense of purpose. 'What's the hurry?' she asked Aurelius.

'The election!' the young Roman replied. 'They're casting their votes for the Consuls: the two men who will rule Rome for the next year.'

'Two *men*,' Alice muttered under her breath. 'What a surprise!'

'The Consuls of Rome are the most powerful people in the known world,' Aurelius declared with a note of pride in his voice. 'My grandfather held the honour some 30 years ago.'

'I'm no expert on history,' Alice said, 'but I thought Rome had an emperor. I didn't realise people voted for their leaders.'

'An emperor?' Aurelius replied. 'No, we despise kings and monarchs of every type here in Rome. Torrents of blood have been spilt when any politician has sought to grab too much power for himself. Here in the Roman Republic, we value democracy.'

Alice bit her lip and kept her thoughts to herself. She may already have said too much to Aurelius about what, from his point of view, was still the future. Her class had studied Ancient Rome in Year 3 and she knew for a fact that it had been ruled by emperors, some of whom were brutal tyrants. She must have arrived in the past at a time before any of those events had happened. She realised she would have to choose her words with great care. As she pondered this realisation, she heard a shout.

'Aurelius!'

A handsome young man in an impressive military uniform was trying to get the attention of her companion.

'Who's that?' Alice whispered, using her hand to cover her mouth.

'That's a friend of my family. Full of charm and intelligence, that one. Father thinks he'll make Consul before his 30th birthday.'

The soldier came over and clasped Aurelius's shoulder, greeting his young friend with a firm handshake.

'Aurelius, my dear boy, it is a joy to see you. And who is this lovely young lady?'

Alice bristled slightly at his patronising tone. 'My name is Alice.'

'It's a privilege to meet you, Alice,' the man replied. 'My name is Julius Caesar.'

Chapter 3

Pronouns and determiners

Chapter overview

If, as they say, good things come in small packages, then you are in for a real treat with this chapter. It's all about small but very useful words. In this chapter we will look at:

• The role of pronouns in replacing nouns.	LKS2	Page 34
• How to identify different types of pronoun.	UKS2	Pages 34–37
• The role of determiners in modifying nouns.	UKS2	Pages 37–38
• How to identify different types of determiner.	UKS2	Pages 38–40
• Ideas and resources to support teaching of these concepts.	LKS2 UKS2	Pages 40–43

In Chapter 2 we explored the different types of noun. In this chapter we will be looking at two of the simplest ways in which we can change and modify nouns: by using pronouns and determiners.

What you need to know

Pronouns and determiners are usually small words but they present a range of possible traps and misconceptions for children. You can worry yourself excessively about the different types and subdivisions of pronoun and determiner, and you'll see all sorts of different ways of categorising them offered in different grammar resources, presented as absolutely objective and indisputable. Try not to worry about these terms – your life is definitely too valuable to be spent agonising over whether a particular word is an indefinite or a distributive pronoun. What matters, both for you and your pupils, is understanding the role of pronouns and determiners and the different sorts of situation in which you might find them.

Replacing nouns with pronouns

Pronouns are words that replace nouns in a sentence. You can see very clearly why they're necessary by considering this sentence:

Ayesha realised that the coat Ayesha had taken home wasn't Ayesha's.

The sentence obviously looks very odd indeed. Once the subject of the sentence, Ayesha, has been introduced at the very beginning, her involvement in the subsequent events is obvious and she doesn't need to be personally identified by name each time. Of course, this sentence is easily fixed:

Ayesha realised that the coat she had taken home wasn't hers.

As before, we have introduced Ayesha as the subject at the very beginning of the sentence. This time, however, we have replaced the other references to her with pronouns: the personal pronoun *she* and the possessive pronoun *hers*.

Before we dive in and look at types of pronoun in more detail, it's worth being aware that children will often get confused between the terms *pronoun* and *proper noun*. The terms sound very similar and pronouns are often used to replace proper nouns. It is worth taking the time to address this head on and make sure that your pupils understand they are different, though related, concepts.

Types of pronoun

DISCLAIMER: We absolutely DO NOT believe that making children memorise the name of every type of pronoun is a good use of their time or yours. However, when teaching about the concept of pronouns generally, it is probably worth your being aware of some of the distinctions in the following table. There is an overlap between pronouns, adjectives and determiners, and some of the words in the table can be classed as all three depending on the situation. We have included them in this chapter as we think that it can be helpful to teach children about them, alongside the pronouns with which they have a lot in common – but that's just our opinion! As always, this is not an exhaustive list and some grammarians would debate some of the terms and distinctions we have included.

Type of pronoun	Usage	Examples	
Personal pronouns (subject)	Subject personal pronouns replace the *subject* of the clause or sentence – the person or thing *doing, being* or *having* the action or state indicated by the *main verb*. For more about subjects, see Chapter 5, page 55.	I You She/he/it We They	**I will help you.** **This is Thomas; he is my friend.**
Personal pronouns (object)	Object personal pronouns replace the *object* of the clause or sentence – the person or thing upon which or upon whom the main verb is being enacted. For more about objects, see Chapter 5, page 55.	Me You Her/him/it Us Them	**I will discuss the matter with them.** **I kicked it into the top corner of the goal.** **Please give the letter to me.**
Possessive pronouns	Possessive pronouns replace nouns that belong to somebody, indicating whom the noun belongs to rather than what the noun actually is. For example, rather than writing 'this is Arda's pencil', I might simply say 'this is **his**'. These are not to be confused with possessive determiners/adjectives such as 'my' and 'your', which modify a noun rather than replacing it (see 'determiners' on page 37).	Mine Yours Hers/his Ours Theirs	**That ring is hers.** **My drawing is better than theirs.** **Yours is the only sensible idea I've heard all day.**
Demonstrative pronouns	Demonstrative pronouns replace nouns that are being indicated (perhaps by being pointed at, for example) by the person speaking or writing. Some of them can also be used as determiners (see 'determiners' on page 37).	This That These Those Them	**Are these yours?** **No, those are mine.** **This has peas in it; I don't like them.**
Indefinite pronouns (many of these can also be used as determiners)	Indefinite pronouns (also referred to as distributive pronouns) refer to non-specific people or things, e.g. '**one** should take care over **everything**'. They are used to make general points that don't only refer to specific nouns. They can replace nouns, e.g. '**Anyone** would find this difficult', or they can modify existing nouns, e.g. '**Any** student would find this difficult.' In the latter instance, they can also be considered to be determiners (see 'determiners' on page 37).	All Another One Any Some Anybody Everybody Somebody Nobody Anyone Everyone Someone No one Anything Everything Something	**Can everybody hear me?** **Some are better than others.** **Nobody should have to experience anything like that.** **Never has so much been owed by so many to so few.**

		Nothing Each Either Much Many Most Neither One Both Few Many Other Others Several	
Interrogative pronouns (whose, what and which can also be used as determiners)	Put simply, interrogative pronouns are used in interrogative sentences. An interrogative sentence is a smug-grammar-person word for 'question'. When, how, what, which, whose and why can all be used as interrogative pronouns. You could tell your class that interrogative pronouns are the words they would use if they were interrogating somebody for information.	Who Whose What Which Why Where When How	**<u>Whose</u> dog is that?** **<u>Why</u> didn't you tell me sooner?** **<u>Where</u> and <u>when</u> will the event take place?** **<u>How</u> and <u>why</u> do you propose to do this?**
Relative pronouns	Relative pronouns are used at the start of relative clauses – clauses that give more information about a noun or a pronoun referred to in a sentence. You can find out more in the chapter about relative clauses on page 103. You may notice that the range of relative pronouns is very similar to the range of interrogative pronouns listed above. The only difference, which leads to a common grammar error, is that 'what' is not a relative pronoun in standard English – one of the words in the list on the right should be used instead.	Who Whose Which Why Where When Why That	**There's the boy <u>who</u> stole my pencil.** **My teacher, <u>whose</u> name is Mrs Campbell, helped me with my work.** **I gave my dad a card <u>that</u> plays music when you open it for his birthday.**

Pronoun controversies

There have been a number of debates over the past few decades about the way we use pronouns, especially in terms of the gender we attach to them. In the past, it was very common for the pronoun 'he' to be used to refer generally to all people. You may notice this in famous old-fashioned sayings such as 'He who laughs last, laughs longest' or 'A bad workman blames his tools.' Different writers have tried different techniques to ensure that the way they use pronouns doesn't come across as sexist. Sometimes this involves using 'she' and 'her' for statements about unspecified people, or using 'they' and 'their' even when referring to a singular but unspecified person:

A wise person always learns from her mistakes.
The successful candidate must present their qualification certificates at the start of the interview.

Our language has evolved over many centuries, and the existence of gendered pronouns perhaps reflects the greater importance people used to place on differentiating between the sexes. We have no firm opinion on the best way to resolve these controversies but they're probably an interesting issue to discuss with older children.

Determiners

While pronouns tend to replace nouns, determiners tend to precede (go before) nouns. Nouns, as we know, are *things*. Determiners tell us (or determine) how many things we are talking about, which particular things we're talking about or whom the things belong to. In technical grammar jargon, we say that they indicate the 'type of reference' made by the noun or noun phrase following them. Apart from the three articles (*the, a* and *an*), most determiners can also be classed as adjectives as they modify nouns and noun phrases. Consider the following list of noun phrases with different determiners at the front:

<u>The</u> white duck

<u>Six</u> white ducks

<u>Any</u> white duck

<u>Which</u> white duck?

<u>This</u> white duck

<u>A</u> white duck

<u>All</u> white ducks

<u>Your</u> white duck

<u>Some</u> white ducks

Needless to say, the sense of what you're saying can change considerably depending on the determiners you choose to deploy. It is worth noting that the possessive form of a noun can also be classed as a determiner when it plays the same role in a noun phrase as the words above, e.g.:

<u>Britain's</u> white ducks
<u>Farmer Giles's</u> white ducks
<u>The park's</u> white ducks

By the end of Year 6, your pupils need to understand the role that determiners play in a sentence. Currently, the National Curriculum divides determiners into the following four categories: articles, possessives, demonstratives and quantifiers. The table below explains how each type of determiner is used and gives some examples.

Types of determiner

Type of determiner	Usage	Examples	
Articles	Using an article indicates to the reader or listener whether you are indicating a particular example of the item described by your noun or noun phrase or whether you are referring to any instance of that item. You can find out more about that distinction on page 39.	The An A	**The** cat sat on the mat. **A** dog buried a bone. **An** emu laid an egg.
Possessive adjectives (these are also classed as determiners)	We use possessive adjectives to show ownership of an item, parts of the body or a relationship between people. Possessive adjectives are not to be confused with possessive pronouns. Whereas a possessive pronoun replaces a noun, for example, 'That is **hers**', possessive adjectives *modify* a noun, e.g. 'That is **her** drink.'	My Your Her/his Our Their	That is <u>my</u> pizza. That is <u>their</u> coat. <u>Her</u> mum runs a B&B. The dog broke <u>its</u> leg.
Demonstrative adjectives (these are also classed as determiners)	Demonstrative adjectives are subtly different to demonstrative pronouns as they modify the noun immediately after them, rather than replacing the noun altogether. It is a distinction worth exploring with children who might say, for example, 'pass me them scissors' instead of 'pass me those scissors'.	This That These Those	Does <u>this</u> cat belong to you? I love <u>those</u> flowers. Do you want <u>these</u> books for your classroom?
Interrogative determiners	Interrogative determiners are subtly different to interrogative pronouns as they modify the noun immediately after them, rather than replacing the noun altogether.	Which Whose What	<u>Which</u> toy would you like? I must find out <u>whose</u> coat this is. <u>What</u> fun this is!
Quantifiers	Quantifiers modify the noun to show how many of something there are. They can be numbers, ordinal numbers or more general terms such as few and many.	One Two Three Etc.	I saw <u>three</u> ships come sailing in. <u>2,894</u> people responded to our survey. I need to borrow <u>five</u> quid.

		First Second Third Etc.	**May is the <u>fifth</u> month of the year.** **Barack Obama was the <u>44th</u> US President.**
		1st 2nd 3rd Etc.	**The <u>first</u> rule of Grammar Club is: 'You do not talk about Grammar Club.'**
		All Another One Any Every Some Each Either Much Most Many Neither Both Few Many Other Others Several	**<u>All</u> swans are birds but <u>most</u> birds are not swans.** **<u>Every</u> possible solution comes with <u>several</u> problems.**

Definite and indefinite articles

Articles are the most common type of determiner and they are among the simplest and most frequently used words in the English language, but they are notoriously difficult to define. Ask someone to give you a definition of 'the' and it's likely they will struggle to do so. This is because, on their own, these words don't really *mean* anything. They just subtly modify the *reference* of the noun or noun phrase that comes after them. *The* is known as the <u>definite article</u>. If someone refers to 'the ostrich', you know they mean one specific ostrich and no other. If they refer to 'the children', you know they mean one specific group of children and no others. It indicates that a specific, definite item or group of items is being referred to. By contrast, *a* and *an* are <u>indefinite articles</u>. If someone refers to 'an ostrich' or 'a child', you know that the reference is indefinite: they could be referring to any ostrich or any child.

If the noun or noun phrase begins with a vowel (*a, e, i, o* or *u*) then you would use the indefinite article *an* to refer to it. If it begins with a consonant (all the other letters of the alphabet), then you would use the indefinite article *a* to refer to it. There are a couple of exceptions to this that you may come across:

- Some acronyms begin with a vowel sound even though the first letter is itself a consonant, e.g. *SOS*. If you tried to write 'SOS' phonetically, you would end up with a strange word beginning with an 'e' that you might spell 'esoess'. For this reason, we would usually talk about sending 'an SOS distress signal' and not 'a SOS distress signal'.

- There are also some words beginning with *h* where it is acceptable to use *an* as the indefinite article, e.g. 'it was an historic occasion'. In general, this is considered appropriate where the stress or emphasis does not fall on the first syllable of the word. So, for example, you could say 'an hotel' because the second syllable of *hotel* is emphasised, but it would not sound right if you said 'an hospital' because the first syllable of *hospital* is emphasised. However, this is exactly the sort of prescriptive nonsense we discourage people from worrying about. It is completely acceptable to use the indefinite article *a* for any countable noun beginning with *h*.

Teaching ideas

The Department for Education is very keen for your pupils to be able to identify pronouns and determiners in sentences, so a lot of these activities are focused around that. However, we believe that the purpose of grammar is to make sense, so we have also included modelled writing you can use with your pupils so that they can see why these elements of grammar are useful. In the current curriculum, pronouns and determiners are both introduced in Key Stage 2, so all of the activities are divided up into upper Key Stage 2 (Years 5 to 6; UKS2) and lower Key Stage 2 (Years 3 to 4; LKS2).

LKS2 What's in the picture?

This is a great way to introduce younger pupils to the concept of determiners. Show them a painting or picture (the busier the better and ideally nothing too abstract!). Ask them to tell their partner what they can see. Listen out for them using determiners, e.g. 'I can see a dog!' or 'I can see three women sitting on the grass.' Explain that while they have been discussing the picture, they have been using determiners. Model how determiners can change the meaning by asking questions about the picture, e.g. *'Put your hand up if you spotted the dog. Notice how the meaning of that sentence changes when I say <u>the</u> dog instead of <u>a</u> dog? It suggests that I have a specific dog in mind, doesn't it?'*

LKS2 *The Planet Without Pronouns*

The Planet Without Pronouns by Justin Martin (2004) is a fantastic book for introducing the importance of pronouns to pupils in lower Key Stage 2. It tells the story of Stanley Sharpleton, who arrives at the planet Krimular. Krimular is a purple planet filled with friendly, six-armed aliens – but absolutely no pronouns! Read the book as a class and discuss what it tells us about the role of pronouns. Your pupils might be inspired to write their own 'planet without pronouns' story!

An or a?

Create a slideshow with a variety of singular nouns or noun phrases, e.g. *animal, egg, class, subject, terrible day, phone call*. Show one word per slide. As each word flashes up on the screen, get your class to shout out 'a' or 'an' to test their knowledge of articles. Don't forget to add a few of the exceptions to this convention (see page 39) to keep them on their toes!

Just a minute!

Choose a pupil to be the first contestant. The aim of the game is for them to speak for one minute about their family without using any personal pronouns. They are out if they accidentally say a pronoun. You then choose a new contestant. This game demonstrates to children how important pronouns are and how they already use them without thinking! Get the rest of the class to listen carefully to the child as they speak to try to catch them out.

Find the pronouns

This activity can be used with both lower Key Stage 2 and upper Key Stage 2 pupils; you just need to ensure that the text is age-appropriate. Give all pupils the same book or extract. Set a timer and ask them to find as many pronouns as they can in two minutes. With lower Key Stage 2, you might want to focus on personal and possessive pronouns, but you can extend your upper Key Stage 2 children by challenging them to find examples of interrogative or relative pronouns.

Write a recipe

Writing recipes is an excellent way to see the importance of determiners, from ensuring that the instructions are in the right order, to making sure that the number of ingredients is correct. Find some examples online (www.greatbritishchefs.com/collections/childrens-baking-recipes is a good place to start) and then get writing your own as a class.

Identifying different determiners

Become determiner detectives! Provide your class with a modelled text and get them to identify the different determiners. To increase the level of challenge, you could add examples of each type of determiner. You can use the following modelled example for this activity. There is a downloadable version of the text available in the online resources for you to project on a whiteboard or print out.

Modelled example

The three witches gathered around the bubbling cauldron. They had been planning this potion for a long time and tonight they finally had hold of the last, vital ingredient. 'BUBBLE, BUBBLE, TOIL AND TROUBLE!' they chanted in unison.

Mary, who was the head of the coven, read out the spell as the others listened carefully. 'First, we must add the tongue of a toad. Second, we stir in three boiled snails. Third, we mix in the eye of a newt.'

The witches added the ingredients and began to stir the mixture, which bubbled and boiled angrily.

'Mary, who shall we test the potion on?' asked one of the witches, nervously.

'The boy, of course.'

'Of course! The boy will make an excellent test case.'

LKS2
UKS2
Create a pronoun cloud

Use an online word cloud generator (we use this one quite a lot: www.wordclouds.com). Have your pupils input as many different pronouns as they can think of, and create a word cloud. This is a great way to assess how much they have remembered about the different sorts of pronoun and, once you have printed their word cloud, you can use it to create a simple but effective display to remind them.

LKS2
UKS2
SHE who laughs last?

As we discussed on page 36, there is currently a debate raging about the use of personal pronouns and gender. With a mature upper Key Stage 2 class, you could explore phrases that use 'he' as the default personal pronoun, e.g. 'He who laughs last, laughs longest.'

Ask your class: *'Should these phrases be updated to use "she" or "they"? Or should we accept that they were from a time when it was very common for the pronoun "he" to be used to refer generally to all people?'*

Encourage your class to really justify their answers. You may want to provide them with sentence starters that model politely agreeing or disagreeing with someone, e.g.:

- 'I take your point but have you considered...'
- 'I have to say I disagree because...'

UKS2
Determiner table

Test your pupils' knowledge of the different types of determiner by challenging them to complete the following table with as many different determiners of each kind as they can. There is

a worksheet version of this table available in the online resources. Simply print and hand out
copies for your pupils to complete.

Articles	Quantifiers	Demonstrative	Interrogative	Possessive

Add the pronouns

UKS2

This is a simple activity that makes the need for pronouns clear. Give each pupil a short extract of text with no pronouns and read it aloud. They will immediately spot the problem and hear how strange the text sounds. Set them the challenge of rewriting the text with pronouns in. See below for a modelled text you could use for this activity. There is a downloadable version of the text available in the online resources for you to project on a whiteboard or print out. You could adapt this activity for lower Key Stage 2 by giving pupils short, separate sentences without pronouns, rather than a paragraph of text. No two children will answer in the exact same way, so choose a couple of pupils to share their work and discuss the decisions they made, e.g. *'Why did you replace that phrase with a pronoun, rather than that one?'*

Modelled text

Jayden left his house and walked into town. Eventually, Jayden stopped when Jayden arrived at Pizza Express. Jayden looked inside and saw his friend Eddie waiting for him. Jayden went into the restaurant, closing the door after Jayden entered. The door shut with a bang. Jayden sat down and greeted Eddie.

'Hi, Eddie. Good to see you,' Jayden said.

'Nice to see you too, Jayden,' Eddie replied.

Jayden and Eddie both looked at the menu. Jayden thought about having spaghetti but, after much deliberation, Jayden decided to have a margarita pizza. Eddie ordered risotto, dough balls, calamari AND garlic bread. Eddie was very hungry!

Chapter 4

Types of verb

Chapter overview

In this chapter we will try to convince you that verbs are not 'doing words'. We will also be looking at:

• How to introduce verbs to children and why they can be hard to define.	**KS1**	Pages 46–47
• How verbs are used to distinguish between the first, second and third person.	**KS1**	Page 47
• How verbs can be arranged and rearranged to create different verb tenses.	**LKS2**	Pages 47–49
• How to use primary auxiliary verbs and modal verbs.	**UKS2**	Pages 49–51
• Ideas and resources to support teaching of these concepts.	**KS1** **LKS2** **UKS2**	Pages 51–54

The verb lies right at the heart of grammar. If your pupils truly understand what verbs are and how they behave in the English language, then half of your job is already done in terms of grammar teaching. Unfortunately, children often don't understand verbs nearly as well as they may appear to. Most children in Year 5 can probably identify the verb in a seemingly mundane sentence like: 'Jack climbed the tree.' Most of them will find it much harder to identify in a genuinely mundane sentence like: 'I'm late.' In this chapter, we're going to hunt down this most elusive but most essential element of English grammar.

What you need to know

It can be helpful to think of nouns and verbs as the matter and energy of grammar. Nouns, as we discussed in Chapter 2, are the things (the objects, ideas, people and places) that a sentence is about. Often, as we discussed in Chapter 3, nouns can be replaced with pronouns. Verbs are the words that get those nouns and pronouns acting and interacting with one another. All the verbs have been underlined in the sentences below:

I <u>stopped</u>.
Ammar and Charlotte <u>should have arrived</u> at school by the time the rain <u>starts</u>.
<u>Finding</u> something difficult <u>is</u> not always as bad as you <u>might think</u>.

These sentences use several different types of verb in several different ways. They are the words that make the nouns and pronouns in the sentence act and interact with each other. However, there is a common temptation when it comes to teaching verbs that we strongly advise against, and that's describing verbs as 'doing words'.

What verbs are not (or why we don't do 'doing words')

When we were at primary school, we were taught that verbs were 'doing words'. Earlier on in our teaching careers, we regularly passed this seriously flawed definition on to our own pupils. We tend to avoid it now, and it's worth taking a moment to explain why.

A 'doing word' is an inadequate explanation of what a verb is for two main reasons. Two of the most commonly used verbs in the English language are *to be* and *to have*. To a child, these don't seem like 'doing words' at all, and relying on that definition will therefore leave them very confused very quickly. Ask yourself, 'Who is doing what?' in the following sentence:

My name <u>is</u> Martha and I <u>have</u> a younger brother.

The two verbs in this sentence are 'is' (the third person singular, simple present tense form of the verb 'to be') and 'have' (the first person singular, simple present tense form of the verb 'to have'). Clearly, however, no one in this sentence is *doing* anything!

The other problem is that, after we tell children a verb is a 'doing word', we generally have to expand this with an even more misleading explanation along the lines of: 'A verb tells you what someone or something in a sentence is doing.' This is simply not true most of the time. Consider this sentence, in which the verb form is underlined:

Luke <u>is finishing</u> his homework.

What is Luke doing? The answer, clearly, is his homework. *Homework* in this sentence is a noun, not a verb. By telling a child that a verb tells you what the subject of the sentence is doing, you risk causing a lot of confusion. Another example would be this sentence, in which the verb is underlined:

Caiden <u>did</u> the dishes.

What did Caiden do? A child would probably, and quite reasonably, say that Caiden did *the dishes*. Again, *dishes* is a noun in this sentence.

We're really sorry, but there are no shortcuts here! Verbs are such a fundamental part of the English language that defining them to someone who doesn't already understand them is no easier than trying to define what numbers are to someone who doesn't already know. However, just like with numbers, it's quite easy to *show* children what verbs are. For that reason, this chapter should be read in conjunction with the next chapter: 'Subject, verb and object', page 55. Trying to teach children what verbs are without teaching the basics of sentence construction is a bit like trying to teach them what numbers are without teaching them to count. Take a look at the 'Teaching ideas' section of this chapter on page 51 for some tips and suggestions about how to *show* children what we mean when we talk about verbs.

Person

Verbs can have first, second or third person forms depending on the subject that accompanies them (the person or thing that is doing, being or having something). The first person is used when the individual speaking or writing is the subject of what is being said, either individually or as part of a larger group (*I, me, we, us*). The second person is used when the person being addressed is the subject of the sentence, either individually or as a larger group (*you*). The third person is used when someone else is the subject of the sentence (*she, he, it, they*). Here are some examples of how verbs can change in the present tense depending on the subject of a clause or sentence.

	Singular (one individual)	Plural (more than one individual)
First person	I <u>am</u> happy. I <u>have</u> a new hat. I <u>sit</u> on this chair.	We <u>are</u> happy. We <u>have</u> new hats. We <u>sit</u> on these chairs.
Second person	You <u>are</u> happy. You <u>have</u> a new hat. You <u>sit</u> on that chair.	You <u>are</u> all happy. You <u>have</u> new hats. You <u>sit</u> on those chairs.
Third person	Jane <u>is</u> happy. Mr Patel <u>has</u> a new hat. The dog <u>sits</u> on that chair.	They <u>are</u> happy. My brothers <u>have</u> new hats. The children <u>sit</u> on those chairs.

Verb tenses and auxiliary verbs

A lot of children (and adults) think that there are three tenses in the English language: past, present and future. Would that it were so simple! (Let's not even get into what tense *that* is.) For the moment, consider the following 12 sentences and the tense they are in:

We wrote a book about grammar.	**(simple past)**
We were writing a book about grammar.	**(past progressive)**
We had written a book about grammar.	**(past perfect)**
We had been writing a book about grammar.	**(past perfect progressive)**
We write a book about grammar.	**(simple present)**
We are writing a book about grammar.	**(present progressive)**
We have written a book about grammar.	**(present perfect)**
We have been writing a book about grammar.	**(present perfect progressive)**
We will write a book about grammar.	**(simple future)**
We will be writing a book about grammar.	**(future progressive)**
We will have written a book about grammar.	**(future perfect)**
We will have been writing a book about grammar.	**(future perfect progressive)**

Each of these tenses alters the meaning of the sentence and each tense has a name. In fact, some have more than one name (you will often see <u>progressive</u> tenses referred to as <u>continuous</u> tenses, for example, but we have stuck to the language of the National Curriculum here). Children need to know some of these names when they sit the grammar, punctuation and spelling assessment in Year 6, but, if you look closely at the list above, you will see that there is actually a fairly neat system, and explaining the whole system may be the easiest way to help older primary pupils remember the terminology.

The first point to notice is that the same four types of tense (simple, perfect, progressive and perfect progressive) appear in each of the past, present and future. If Ebenezer Scrooge had been haunted by grammar pedants, this is probably how they'd have approached their task! All four of these tenses can be made using variations of the main verb in the sentence (in this case 'to write') but most are formed using verb phrases (see Chapter 12, page 121) that combine a version of the main verb (called a <u>participle</u>) with variations of the verbs 'to have' and 'to be' (called <u>primary auxiliary verbs</u>). Auxiliary verbs can sometimes be thought of as 'helper verbs' and these primary auxiliary verbs help to form a tense alongside the main verb.

We <u>have been writing</u> a book about grammar.

'We' is the subject of this sentence and 'a book about grammar' is the object (again, see Chapter 5, page 55, for more on this). The verb phrase is formed using two primary auxiliary verbs, *have* and *been*, with the present participle form of 'to write', *writing*.

To indicate that a clause or sentence is written in the future tense, we add the modal verb 'will':

The rabbit will have eaten all the cabbages.

In this sentence, 'the rabbit' is the subject and 'all the cabbages' is the object. The verb phrase is formed by the modal verb *will*, the auxiliary verb *have* and the past participle form of 'to eat': *eaten*. There is more about modal verbs in the next section on page 50.

First, let's look at the types of tense in more detail.

Types of tense

<u>Simple tenses</u> are general and non-specific. They simply indicate actions or states of affairs that took place in the past, that take place in the present or that will take place in the future. They consist of the main verb in its present tense form for the simple present, in its past tense form for the simple past or accompanied by the modal verb 'will' for the simple future.

Simple past: I <u>walked</u> to school.
Simple present: I <u>walk</u> to school.
Simple future: I <u>will walk</u> to school.

<u>Progressive tenses</u> indicate actions or states of affairs that were, are or will be in progress at the time you're talking or writing about. They were, are or will be in the process of happening at that moment. They are formed using an auxiliary verb derived from the verb 'to be' and the present participle form of the main verb.

Past progressive: I <u>was walking</u> to school.
Present progressive: I <u>am walking</u> to school.
Future progressive: I <u>will be walking</u> to school.

<u>Perfect tenses</u> indicate actions or states of affairs that had been, have been or will have been completed at the time you're talking about. The 'present perfect' can confuse people as it often appears to be indicating something that happened in the past. However, it is classed as a present tense because it communicates the fact that, in the present moment, a particular action or state of affairs <u>has been</u> completed. Perfect tenses are formed using an auxiliary verb derived from the verb 'to have' and the past participle form of the main verb.

Past perfect: I <u>had walked</u> to school.
Present perfect: I <u>have walked</u> to school.
Future perfect: I <u>will have walked</u> to school.

<u>Perfect progressive tenses</u>, as the name suggests, are a combination of the perfect and the progressive tense. They indicate actions or states of affairs that had been in progress up until the moment you're talking about. They are formed using an auxiliary verb derived from the verb 'to have', an auxiliary verb derived from the verb 'to be' and the present participle form of the main verb.

Past perfect progressive: I <u>had been walking</u> to school.
Present perfect progressive: I <u>have been walking</u> to school.
Future perfect progressive: I <u>will have been walking</u> to school.

Modal verbs

Modal verbs are a class of auxiliary verb. However, whereas primary auxiliary verbs tend to affect tense, modal verbs modify the actual meaning of the main verb in a sentence. They often give the reader an idea of how likely it is that the action or state of affairs indicated by the verb will actually come to pass. There are nine modal verbs commonly used in English, some of which are quite similar in meaning, and all of which have contracted negations (see Chapter 7, page 77), although 'mayn't' is seldom used these days. These nine modal verbs are:

Can/can't
Could/couldn't
May/mayn't (may not)
Might/mightn't
Must/mustn't
Shall/shan't
Should/shouldn't
Will/won't
Would/wouldn't

In the last section, we looked at the way 'will' is used to indicate something taking place in the future. Most of these modal verbs can be used to make verb phrases in several different tenses:

I <u>could</u> have done a better job on this.
She <u>must</u> be wondering where we are.
I probably <u>shouldn't</u> have any more cake.

Most of this is pretty instinctive and doesn't tend to cause pupils too many problems. However, there is one error that children and adults alike often make that gets corrected by teachers thousands of times a day right across the English-speaking world: following a modal verb with the word 'of', e.g.:

~~I should of told you sooner.~~

This happens because when we add a modal verb to a present or future perfect verb phrase, we can contract the modal verb and the word 'have'. *Could have done* becomes *could've done*, *should have known* becomes *should've known*, etc. Even when we don't write the words this way, it's how we almost always pronounce them. To children's ears, the contracted remnants of the word 'have' are indistinguishable from the word 'of'. Teachers find themselves trying to explain this to children again and again but, until they've understood at least some of the grammar points covered in the last two sections, they're likely to keep on making the same mistake.

Teaching ideas

According to the National Curriculum, verbs should be taught from Key Stage 1 upwards. Keep reading to find a range of activities for both key stages.

Clap when you hear

KS1

Read a story to the class and ask the children to clap when they hear a verb. You might want to use the modelled writing on page 53 for this activity or a quality picture book that your pupils enjoy.

Balloon verb game

KS1

There are lots of fantastic grammar resources online. Get this game up on your interactive whiteboard and have different children come and find the verbs to assess whether they have understood what verbs are: www.softschools.com/language_arts/grammar/verb/balloon_game.

Past or present

KS1

This is a quick and easy way to assess whether pupils have understood past and present tense. Give each table of pupils one of the sets of cards below. There is a printable version of each set in the online resources, so simply print copies of the set you wish to use and cut it up into cards. Explain that the pupils have to sort the cards into past and present tense. The three sets of cards vary by level of challenge according to the number of irregular verbs included.

Level 1

Joke	Waited	Trim	Liked
Jumped	Read	Coped	Like
Talk	Sing	Cut	Hopped
Talked	Hope	Walked	Crop

Swing	Stopped	Climb	Mixed
Shopped	Stop	Climbed	Fix

Level 2

Believe	Made	Went	Take
Come	Ate	Felt	Got
Gave	Find	Think	Tell
Become	Show	Leave	Question
Bought	Begin	Kept	Hold
Held	Keep	Began	Brought

Level 3

Tried	Found	Look	Break
Sang	Had	Write	Lit
Swam	Went	Light	Extinguish
Drove	Did	Grew	Drank
Taught	Scream	Lay	Stole
Learnt	Cried	Broke	Dug

KS1 Verb charades

A twist on the classic game of charades. Instead of miming film or book titles, pupils have to mime out different verbs. Initially, you might want to keep it simple by encouraging the children to choose actions such as to swim, to run or to eat, but you can make this game more challenging by giving pupils verbs like to believe or to hope.

Replace the word

KS1

LKS2

UKS2

The simplest way to introduce children to the concept of verbs is to give them sentences and point out the verb (without calling it the verb to begin with), before asking them to think of words they could replace it with. In most cases, they will be able to think of alternatives that have very similar meanings (synonyms) and alternatives that completely change the meaning of the sentence. They may start to notice that the tense of the sentence can change depending on the word they choose. It's important to point out that there are also plenty of words that cannot be put in place of the verb, as the sentence would no longer make any sense. If children do this several times with several different sentences (you may want to use the modelled writing below to help with this), then they will quickly build up a *sense* of what sort of words verbs are and what sort of words they are not. This will be far more helpful than any definition you can give them for the concept of a verb.

Modelled writing

One cat dozed quietly on the sofa, while the other wandered around the house. They had gobbled down their lunch and were already thinking about dinner. Suddenly, they heard the sound of a key turning in the lock. They both raced into the hallway as I stepped in through the door. They ran between my legs, tripping me up as I walked to the kitchen.

Venn diagrams

KS1

LKS2

UKS2

Ask your pupils to draw three overlapping circles, labelling one 'verbs', another 'nouns' and the third 'adjectives'. Provide them with a selection of words and ask them to place them in the appropriate places on the Venn diagram. Discuss how some words fall into more than one category depending on the context. This activity could be modified for Key Stage 1 by just using a Venn diagram with two circles showing, for example, verbs and nouns.

Switch the verb

LKS2

UKS2

Write a simple sentence on the board. Alter the level of challenge by choosing this carefully. For example:

Jessica won the race.

Challenge pairs of children to find as many different verbs as they can that could replace 'won' but still make sense in the sentence, even if it changes the meaning. Discuss how the meaning of the sentence changes with the verb, e.g.:

Jessica lost the race.

Jessica entered the race.

Jessica finished the race.

Jessica endured the race.

Jessica enjoyed the race.

Jessica relished the race.

Verb kung fu

This will probably be most effective and more fun in pairs and groups. Give each group a short passage containing lots of verbs of different types (the modelled writing below might be useful). Agree a martial-arts-style move that goes with each type of verb, e.g. a high kick for main verbs, a karate chop for modal verbs and a punch for primary auxiliary verbs. You could change the move depending on whether the verb has a first-, second- or third-person subject. The group then read out their passage, performing the correct moves at the right times.

> ### Modelled writing
>
> I should have realised it was never going to be this simple. When I had first thought about becoming a spy, I had imagined my whole life would be a series of exciting and glamorous adventures. I couldn't have been more wrong. I now found myself imprisoned in Professor Iorek Van Gambles' castle and I could see no way to escape. Just at the moment when I had given up all hope, I realised that I had been carrying a device that would help me escape the whole time. Why didn't I think of this earlier?
>
> 'I must be quick,' I thought to myself, as I reached into my pocket and pulled out the laser-cutting yoyo I had been given before I left HQ.

Shoulda, woulda, coulda

You can use almost any book for this. Choose a character facing a dilemma and ask pupils:

- What **can** this character do?
- What **must** this character do?
- What **should** this character do?
- What **could** this character do?
- What **would** YOU do if you were in this character's position?

This activity helps pupils to consolidate their knowledge about modal verbs by using them in context. It will inevitably lead to a discussion about the subtle differences between verbs like can and could. *(Playing the Beverley Knight song is optional.)*

Chapter 5

Subject, verb and object

Chapter overview

If a child's writing doesn't 'sound right' then it could mean they haven't understood subject–verb agreement. Don't worry though, we're here to help! In this chapter we will look at:

• How to identify the subject and verb in a sentence.	**LKS2**	Pages 56–57
• Understanding subject and verb agreement.	**KS1**	Page 57
• The distinction between direct and indirect objects.	**UKS2**	Pages 57–58
• Subject and object pronouns.	**UKS2**	Pages 58–59
• Ideas and resources to support teaching of these concepts.	**LKS2** **UKS2**	Pages 59–62

The concept of 'subject, verb and object' sounds very complicated and sophisticated, and we can recall hearing appalled colleagues question why on Earth the Department for Education had thought it an appropriate topic for the primary curriculum when the spelling, punctuation and grammar assessments were first introduced. However, it's actually a very basic idea and it's one that even very young children understand innately. From the moment we learn to use 'I' and 'me' correctly, we have in fact developed an understanding of the difference between the subject and the object of a clause or sentence. Being able to identify the subject is particularly useful and makes it much easier to understand some of the more abstract ideas in grammar that we'll be looking at later on.

What you need to know

Making sense in English usually involves saying or writing clauses and sentences. In this chapter, we are going to look at 'simple sentences'. Don't let the name deceive you: a simple sentence can be very sophisticated and it can be fairly long. In grammar, a sentence is described as 'simple' if it contains only one clause. We will deal more with clauses and how to create more complex sentences in Part Two of the book but, for the moment, we are going to stick with simple sentences. Because of their misleading name, teachers often skip over simple sentences and don't spend as much time on them as they really should. In fact, some of the ideas and terminology in this chapter are really quite complex and you probably won't want to go into all of it in detail with your pupils, even in Year 6. However, the distinction between subject and object is part of the primary curriculum and it can't hurt to be a few steps ahead so that you can answer the questions children will inevitably ask.

Subject and verb

To create a simple sentence, you usually need to take a noun or a pronoun (a person, a place, an item or an idea: the <u>subject</u> of your clause or sentence) and tell your reader or listener what the subject is doing, having or being. The very simplest way to do this is to combine your subject with a <u>verb</u> or a <u>verb phrase</u>:

Justice prevailed.
> *What prevailed? Justice. Therefore 'justice' is the subject of this sentence.*
> *What did justice do? It prevailed. Therefore 'prevailed' is the verb in this sentence.*

You smell!
> *Who smells? You do! Therefore 'you' are the subject of the sentence.*
> *What do you do? You smell! Therefore 'smell' is the verb in this sentence.*

The film hasn't finished.
> *What hasn't finished? The film. Therefore 'the film' is the subject of the sentence.*
> *What hasn't the film done? It hasn't finished. Therefore 'hasn't finished' is the verb phrase.*

These very simple sentences communicate very simple ideas. Each is composed of a subject and a verb phrase and nothing else. The subject and verb phrase are the fundamental building blocks of sentences. Without them, a sentence is not a sentence. Sometimes, the subject of a sentence can be a longer noun phrase, more than one noun or more than one pronoun. It does not have to be a single word, e.g.:

<u>**Justice and common sense**</u> prevailed.
<u>**You and I**</u> smell.
<u>**This long, boring film**</u> hasn't finished.

It is also worth being aware that the verb phrase in a simple sentence can sometimes be quite long. Consider these examples:

They <u>**hadn't expected to arrive**</u> so soon.
This <u>**may not turn out to have been**</u> such a good idea.
Leon <u>**was hoping he might be able to make**</u> some new friends.

It is beyond the scope of this book to go into detail about all these different constructions and the grammatical terms we would use to describe them. However, it is important to be aware that there are very many different types of verb phrase, and examining examples like these is an interesting way to encourage more able children in Key Stage 2 to reflect on how they can use different verb forms to give their writing precision and clarity.

Subject–verb agreement

The verb form in a sentence has to 'agree' with the subject. That is to say, the version of the verb that is used must be appropriate to the subject. Often the verb will be different depending on whether the subject is referred to in the first, second or third person and whether it is singular or plural. Consider these examples:

I like cheese.
Harry likes cheese.
Harry and Agam like cheese.

You will sometimes hear children (and adults) deviating from the usual conventions of standard English when it comes to subject–verb agreement. Two common examples are:

~~You was talking too loudly.~~
instead of
~~You were talking too loudly.~~

~~He don't want it.~~
instead of
He doesn't want it.

While it is of course important to respect the fact that spoken English varies from region to region and dialect to dialect, our aim as teachers is to teach children to write in standard English. It is therefore probably right that we ensure that children know the standard verb forms to use in these instances, even as we understand the fact that they may speak differently at home.

Direct and indirect objects

As well as a subject and a verb phrase, many clauses and sentences also include a direct object. The direct object of a clause or sentence is the person or thing that undergoes the action denoted by the verb. In other words, the object is the person or thing *to which the verb is done*, e.g.:

Mrs Dalton painted the fence.
What did Mrs Dalton paint? She painted the fence. Therefore 'the fence' is the object.

I like Adam.
Who do I like? I like Adam. Therefore 'Adam' is the object.

The teacher submitted her letter of resignation.

What did the teacher submit? She submitted her letter of resignation. Therefore 'her letter of resignation' is the object.

All of the objects in the examples we've seen so far are <u>direct objects</u>. They are the people or things *upon whom the verb acts*. However, some sentences and some clauses contain both a direct object and an <u>indirect object</u>. The indirect object is the recipient of the direct object – the person or thing to whom the direct object is given or applied. Look at these examples:

He gave <u>the ball</u> an almighty kick.

What did he give? He gave an almighty kick. Therefore 'an almighty kick' is the direct object.
What was given an almighty kick? The ball. Therefore 'the ball' is the indirect object.

My aunt sent <u>me</u> a birthday card.

What did my aunt send? She sent a birthday card. Therefore 'a birthday card' is the direct object.
Who was sent a birthday card? I was. Therefore 'me' is the indirect object.

Laila showed <u>the teacher</u> her work.

What did Laila show? She showed her work. Therefore 'her work' is the direct object.
Who was shown the work? Her teacher. Therefore 'her teacher' is the indirect object.

All of these sentences could be rewritten so that the indirect object appears in a prepositional phrase (or prepositional complement) at the end of the sentence, i.e. a phrase introduced by a preposition like 'to'. However, you will notice that writing them this way sometimes sounds clumsier and less elegant:

Subject	Verb	Direct object	Prepositional phrase
He	gave	an almighty kick	to the ball.
My aunt	sent	a birthday card	to me.
Laila	showed	her work	to the teacher.

You can read more about complements in Appendix 5, page 189.

Subject and object pronouns

You have actually had a vague understanding of subject and object for as long as you could talk, and we can prove it. *I* and *me* are personal pronouns and, obviously, their meaning is pretty much the same. However, *I* is used when the speaker or writer is the subject of a sentence and *me* is used when the speaker is the object of the sentence. We apply this convention without thinking about it hundreds of times a day:

He gave <u>me</u> the ball.
<u>I</u> gave him the ball.
<u>I</u> like her.
She likes <u>me</u>.

The only time this ever causes real confusion for native English speakers is when we combine 'I' and another person or item to form the subject or object of a sentence:

Dhiya and <u>I</u> played football.
The letter was addressed to Andrew and <u>me</u>.

The convention is just the same in these instances but, of course, a lot of people have never even noticed that it exists because they've never thought about sentences in terms of subjects and objects. If the person speaking is part of the subject, then they would use 'I'. If the person speaking is part of the object, they would use 'me'. The same logic applies to other personal pronouns too:

<u>He</u> and his dog saw <u>us</u>.
<u>We</u> saw <u>him</u> and his dog.
<u>They</u> like <u>her</u>.
<u>She</u> likes <u>them</u>.

The other thorny issue surrounding subject and object pronouns centres on the distinction between 'who' and 'whom' when used as relative or interrogative pronouns. Traditionally, it has been considered acceptable for 'who' to be used as the subject of a sentence and 'whom' to be used as the object of the sentence, e.g.:

Who are you?
To whom shall I address my complaint?

To be perfectly honest, this 'rule' is not observed by most people anymore, if it ever was, so it's far from clear that it is actually a rule at all. As we explained in the introduction, grammar is an attempt to describe the way people write and speak in standard English and to reflect on the different effects our words can have by being presented in different forms. Using *who* and *whom* 'correctly' is simply not an important part of that. Don't worry about it!

Teaching ideas

Subject, verb and object is not something we would expect to be covered in Key Stage 1. By all means have a conversation about identifying the verb and who/what is doing the verb when reading with younger children, but that is probably as much as they need at this point. For this reason, these teaching ideas are aimed at Key Stage 2 children. When teaching subject, verb and object, the main points you will need to get across to your pupils are:

1. How to identify the subject, verb and object in a sentence.

2. Understanding that the subject may not be one word but could be a noun phrase, e.g. 'the oldest dragon'.

3. Which verb form to use for the subject (subject–verb agreement).

4. Not all sentences have an object.

The following activities are a good place to start.

LKS2 ## Get arty

This would work particularly well with children in lower Key Stage 2 who are first being introduced to subject, verb and object. To begin with, keep it simple and choose paintings with people as subjects (*American Gothic* by Grant Wood is a great one for this, for example). Show the class the painting and ask them to identify:

- Who or what does the action in the painting? (Subject)
- What is the action? (Verb)
- Who/what is affected by the action? (Object)

For example:

- *Mona Lisa is watching the painter. (Mona Lisa is the subject. 'Watching' is the verb. The painter is the object.)*
- *The man is holding a pitch fork. (The man is the subject. 'Holding' is the verb. The pitch fork is the object.)*

Challenge your pupils to write as many sentences as they can about the paintings and identify the subject, verb and object in each one.

 LKS2 ## Subject–verb agreement gap fill

 UKS2

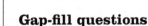 Present pupils with the following simple gap-fill questions. Read the sentences with your class and identify whether the subject of the sentence is plural or singular. Then have the discussion about which form of the verb should go in the gap. There is a worksheet version of this task in the online resources for you to print and hand out.

Gap-fill questions

Ali and Mo <u>is/are</u> sitting on the sofa.
Gary <u>like/likes</u> to eat Mexican food.
Antonia <u>walk/walks</u> to 10 Downing Street.
The boys <u>play/plays</u> together.

The dog chew/chewed/chewing his bone.
The baby sleeps/sleep/slept last night.
Yasmin are/is going out tonight.
There are/is four crisps left.
Dave was/were disappointed that Arsenal lost the match.

Identifying subject/verb/object

Display a series of simple sentences up on the board. You could use the following list of sentences or, alternatively, the short extract if you want to increase the level of challenge. There are versions of both the list and the extract in the online resources to save you typing them up. Read the sentences or extract aloud as a class and introduce the task: to identify the subject, verb and object. Agree on a key, e.g. colour the object in red, the subject in blue and the verb in purple, and then let children work independently, identifying the different parts of the sentence. If you have a Year 6 class who are ready for it, then they could also identify any complements and adjuncts. For more information on complements and adjuncts head over to Appendix 5, page 189.

Sentences for identifying the subject, verb and object

The black, fluffy cat ate the fresh fish.
Ali and Mo saw their friend.
Jack wrote a letter.
The teacher read out the register.
After she finished her coffee, Antonia completed a crossword. *(There are two clauses in this sentence so have a go at identifying the subject, verb and object in both.)*

Short extract

Zuzanna ran home excitedly. Today was her birthday! On the way home, she saw her friend Blake. He gave her a birthday present. Zuzanna ripped the wrapping paper in excitement. Inside, she found a new notebook. She thanked Blake and continued her journey. She saw her mum waiting on the doorstep. She was holding a bunch of green balloons.

Word sort

Provide your pupils with the following simple table with the headings 'Subject', 'Verb' and 'Object' at the top. (Don't worry – there is a worksheet in the online resources you can print out for this.) Read the example at the top of the grid: 'I ate a biscuit.' Explain that when you read across each row of the grid you create a simple sentence. Provide your pupils with a range of words and ask them to put them into the subject/verb/object columns to create simple sentences. The suggested words below are included in the worksheet online to avoid you typing them up.

Subject–verb–object table

Subject	Verb	Object
I	ate	a biscuit

Suggested words to sort into the table

watched	the boy	went
ate	painted	the fish
they	a picture	the cats
a film	the bag	Jessica
the children	home	carried

UKS2 History

Once your class have a basic understanding of subject, verb and object, you can consolidate it in other lessons by asking pupils to identify the subject, verb and object in non-fiction books or on websites about your subject. For example, in history, they might read, 'Henry VIII married Anne Boleyn.' You don't have to labour the point but just a brief pause to ask, 'Who or what is the subject of that sentence?' will reinforce the concept.

Chapter 6
Adjectives and adverbs

Chapter overview

In this chapter we will mainly be ranting about adjectives. We will also concede that they probably do need to be taught, so we will also look at:

• The role of different types of adjective in modifying nouns.	**KS1**	Pages 64–65
• Absolute, comparative and superlative adjectives.	**LKS2**	Pages 65–68
• How we instinctively apply the 'order of adjectives'.	**UKS2**	Pages 68–69
• The role of different types of adverb in modifying verbs and adjectives.	**LKS2**	Pages 69–71
• Ideas and resources to support teaching of these concepts.	**KS1** **LKS2** **UKS2**	Pages 72–76

Before we start, a rant about adjectives

'Eschew all those beastly adjectives.' Roald Dahl (1980)

I think we can all agree that children need to learn to identify and use adjectives. When used effectively, adjectives add detail, create humour and paint a clear picture in the reader's mind.

While we understand why we have to teach children about adjectives, we do not understand why we teach children about adjectives as often as we do. Primary school schemes of work appear to be full of endless lessons on describing settings and characters. This has sent out the message to a generation of children that adjectives are the hallmark of good writing and should be used at every opportunity. Oh and not just any old adjectives like big, small, hot and cold. No, we teach children that they need to be using longer adjectives or 'WOW words' as we call them.

As a result, teachers end up reading about the ancient, decrepit man and the boiling, scorching sun or writing sentences like: '*The big, grey elephant walked through the jungle.*' For most people, the word 'elephant' immediately conjures up the image of a big, grey animal that lives in a jungle. Adjectives change, or *modify*, the meaning of nouns. The picture the reader has of an elephant is utterly unchanged by adding 'big' and 'grey' to the front of it. These adjectives are not modifying the noun and they do not work in the sentence. In fact, unless the elephant in question is small and red, the most effective way of describing an elephant is simply by using the word 'elephant'.

So yes, teach your class about adjectives and how to use them but emphasise the importance of being sparing with adjectives. When you're reading their work, challenge them to justify the adjectives they have chosen.

OK, rant over. We can now begin.

What you need to know

Adjectives and adverbs are both <u>modifiers</u>: words that alter or affect the meanings of other words. Adjectives modify nouns or noun phrases whereas adverbs modify verbs. However, adverbs can also be used to modify adjectives – how terribly confusing! Let's take them one at a time.

Adjectives

Adjectives modify nouns and pronouns. When you introduce adjectives to children in Key Stage 1, the examples they will come up with are often words to describe colour, size or shape, e.g.:

The sun is <u>yellow</u>.
I saw a <u>big</u> car.

Then we start to move on to more detailed descriptive modifications such as:

I had a <u>relaxing</u> holiday.
The result was <u>unanimous</u>.
<u>Obsequious</u> behaviour is frowned upon in this organisation.

However, in teaching adjectives, teachers often neglect to explain that some far more commonly used words than those mentioned above are also adjectives. Let's look at some of these.

Quantifying adjectives

Adjectives can also describe quantity or numerical order, e.g.:

I have <u>three</u> cats.
He was the <u>first</u> person in the line.

Most children come to learn adjectives as 'describing words'. Before we move on, a little suggestion about that.

Modifiers not describing words

It is understandable that we often introduce adjectives to young children as 'describing words'. However, it is probably a good idea to start using the term *modifier* rather than *describing word* as soon as possible. A modifier alters, clarifies or qualifies the meaning of a word. Think about the following example:

There are <u>six</u> cups in the cupboard.

In this sentence, the word *six* is an adjective. It tells you how many cups there are in the cupboard but it does not describe the size, shape or colour of them.

Comparative adjectives

As the name suggests, comparative adjectives are used to draw comparisons. When using comparative adjectives, we often use 'than' in between the adjective and the nouns, pronouns or noun phrases that are being compared, e.g.:

The sunflowers are <u>taller</u> than the rose bush.
He seems <u>happier</u> than he used to be.
She is <u>stronger</u> than him.

Most comparative adjectives are formed by adding the *-er* suffix, as explained in the table below.

If the adjective...	To make the comparative form:
Ends in a vowel and consonant, e.g.: **Big** **Mad**	Double the consonant and add *-er*, e.g.: **Big → Bigger** **Mad → Madder**
Ends in consonant and 'y', e.g.: **Busy** **Happy**	Change the 'y' to an 'i' and add *-er*, e.g.: **Busy → Busier** **Happy → Happier**
Ends in 'e', e.g.: **Free** **Large**	Add *-r*, e.g.: **Free → Freer** **Large → Larger**
For all other adjectives, e.g.: **Old** **Rich**	Add *-er*, e.g.: **Old → Older** **Rich → Richer**

The common exceptions, or irregular forms, are listed out in the table on the following page.

Adjective	Comparative
Good	Better
Bad	Worse
Little	Less
Much	More
Far	Further

For example:

She is <u>better</u> at maths than he is.
He is <u>worse</u> than me at football.
I have <u>less</u> time than him.

For some adjectives, including any that are of three syllables or more, we need to use 'more' to create the comparative form, e.g.:

She is <u>more popular</u> than I am.
That book is <u>more interesting</u> than the one we read yesterday.

Superlative adjectives

Superlative adjectives are used to draw comparisons when there are more than two things being compared. For example:

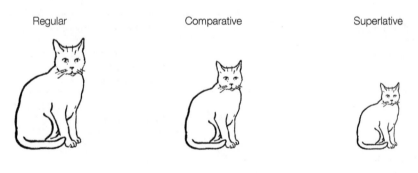

Regular   Comparative   Superlative

This cat is <u>small</u>.   **This cat is <u>smaller</u>.**   **This is the <u>smallest</u> cat.**

Other examples include:

She is the <u>tallest</u> in the class.
This is the <u>simplest</u> way of doing it.
Our marrow was the <u>heaviest</u> at the fair.

Most superlative adjectives are formed by adding the -*est* suffix as follows:

If the adjective...	To make the superlative form:
Ends in a vowel and consonant, e.g.: **Big** **Mad**	Double the consonant and add -*est*, e.g.: **Big → Biggest** **Mad → Maddest**
Ends in consonant and 'y', e.g.: **Busy** **Happy**	Change the 'y' to an 'i' and add -*est*, e.g.: **Busy → Busiest** **Happy → Happiest**
Ends in 'e', e.g.: **Free** **Large**	Add -*st*, e.g.: **Free → Freest** **Large → Largest**
For all other adjectives (that are not in the list of exceptions), e.g.: **Old** **Rich**	Add -*est*, e.g.: **Old → Oldest** **Rich → Richest**

As with comparative adjectives, there are some common irregular forms:

Adjective	Superlative
Good	Best
Bad	Worst
Little	Least
Much	Most
Far	Furthest/Farthest

For example:

I am the <u>best</u> at tennis.
That was the <u>worst</u> film I've seen this year.
I'd had the <u>least</u> practice out of everyone in the class.

Sometimes, to create the superlative form of an adjective, we use most or least, rather than changing the adjective itself. For example:

The Prime Minister was the <u>most famous</u> person he had ever met.

In this sentence, 'most famous' is the superlative adjective but, when broken down, 'famous' is the adjective and 'most' is acting as an adverb. (We will move on to adverbs in a couple of pages' time but if you really can't wait then head over to page 69 now.)

Absolute adjectives

In contrast to comparative and superlative adjectives, absolute adjectives cannot take the superlative or comparative form. Words such as perfect, dead, unique, basic and obvious are, in most cases, absolute adjectives.

It is easier to understand the concept of an absolute adjective when you already know about comparative and superlative adjectives, so it would make sense to introduce them to children in that order.

Compound adjectives

A compound adjective is an adjective that is made up of more than one word. High-risk, part-time, ill-equipped and warm-blooded are examples of compound adjectives.

We often use a hyphen to link the words in a compound adjective. The conventions for doing so are fairly complex but, at primary level, children simply need to understand that the hyphen combines two words to form a single adjective. Here are some examples:

The beautiful <u>pea-green</u> boat.
The cat let out an <u>ear-piercing</u> screech.

Articles

Often overlooked, articles, *a*, *the* and *an*, are adjectives because they modify the nouns that they precede. Have a look at the following sentences:

<u>A</u> man appeared in the doorway.
<u>The</u> man appeared in the doorway.

In that second sentence, the change of article modifies the noun 'man' and indicates that we know who the man is. Just a little note: the current National Curriculum refers to articles as determiners, so you will find plenty more on articles on page 37.

Adjective pronouns and determiners

There are several types of adjective that are often thought of as a type of pronoun or determiner, such as demonstrative adjectives (*this, that, those,* etc.), possessive adjectives (*his, her, their,* etc.), interrogative adjectives (*what, where, who,* etc.) and distributive adjectives (*every, either, any,* etc.) All of these words can, in different ways, be used to modify nouns. However, we had to make a choice, so we have included them in the chapter on pronouns and determiners (page 33). We think that teaching children about these sorts of adjectives alongside pronouns and determiners will ultimately be less confusing for primary-aged children, even if that judgement incurs the wrath of many hardcore adjective fans!

Order of adjectives

Even if you don't know the order of adjectives, you do. Look at this sentence:

~~The green, big dragon was sitting in its cave.~~

If a child writes this, you will think to yourself, 'No, it's the *big, green* dragon, not the *green, big* dragon!'

Why? Well, this is pretty weird. For those of us who grew up with English as a first language, the order of adjectives is almost innate knowledge. Without realising it, when you use multiple adjectives to describe a noun, you list them in the following order.

Order	Describe	For example
1	Opinion	*magnificent, enthralling, terrible*
2	Size	*tiny, huge, short*
3	Physical quality	*smooth, thick, bristly*
4	Shape	*square, round, hexagonal*
5	Age	*ancient, young, newborn*
6	Colour	*green, black, orange*
7	Origin	*British, Greek, Dutch*
8	Material	*fabric, metal, wooden*
9	Purpose	*cleaning, hammering, cooking*

So, I might say:

I have a useful, shiny, blue, Swedish, plastic, shopping bag.

If you start messing about with the order of adjectives, things go pear-shaped very quickly:

~~I have a shopping, blue, plastic, useful, shiny, Swedish bag.~~

While this may be the first time you have seen that list, it is likely you already had a sense of it. It is how you know to say 'the big, red bus' not 'the red, big bus' and why you might describe your handbag as being made of 'soft, Italian leather' not 'Italian, soft leather'.

The majority of the pupils you teach will also be able to 'hear' which order sounds right but not all will be able to, particularly if English is not their first language. For this reason, it is worth introducing children to the order of adjectives, and it can be introduced as young as Key Stage 1 – you could start by singing the song 'The Little Green Frog' as a class and discussing why the words are said in that particular order.

Adverbs

Adverbs modify the verb in the sentence, so it makes sense that you should make sure your class know about verbs before you try to teach adverbs. (For more information on verbs and how to teach them, turn to page 45.) Adverbs tell us more about how, where, when or how often an action is carried out, e.g.:

I <u>quickly</u> ate my food.
He was going <u>somewhere</u>.
I am going to the cinema <u>tomorrow</u>.
I <u>completely</u> failed to answer the question.
She <u>rarely</u> eats meat.

Let's look at these five categories in a bit more detail.

Adverbs of manner

Adverbs of manner tell you more about how an action was carried out. These are the adverbs we first introduce to children, and most adverbs of manner end in the suffix *-ly*, e.g. *softly, clearly, fluently, happily*, etc.

He whistled <u>happily</u> to himself.

It is important that we don't tell children that all adverbs end in *-ly*. In years gone by, we might have referred to adverbs as '-ly words'. Try to avoid this because there are as many adverbs that don't end in *-ly* as there are those that do.

Adverbs of place

These adverbs tell us more about where the action took place, e.g. *outside, there, here, somewhere, inside*, etc.

Adverbs of time

As you have probably worked out by now, these adverbs tell you more about when the action took place, e.g. *yesterday, tomorrow, later, next*, etc.

Adverbs of degree

Adverbs of degree tell us about the intensity of something – the degree to which it is happening. Any time you comment that someone is moving too slowly, or that a child in your class isn't working hard enough in lessons, you are using adverbs of degree, e.g.:

You are speaking <u>too</u> quietly.
You are running <u>very</u> fast.

Common adverbs of degree are *too, enough, very* and *extremely*. They are not to be confused with adverbs of frequency. Which is where we're going next.

Adverbs of frequency

Adverbs of frequency tell you how often the verb is happening, e.g.:

I brush my teeth <u>regularly</u>.
I <u>never</u> eat meat.
I <u>usually</u> go to bed at 9.00 pm.

When teaching adverbs of frequency, have the discussion about what these words mean. So what is the difference between *doing something rarely* compared to *seldom doing something*? Does somebody who *frequently* eats out have more meals out than someone who *often* eats out? This is almost entirely subjective but will prompt some interesting discussion and give you a chance to assess that your pupils really understand what these adverbs mean. Turn to page 72 for an activity on teaching adverbs of frequency.

Adverbials

This is a word that you need to understand. The <u>fronted adverbial</u> has become the poster boy of the current English curriculum and people seem to talk about it a lot! An adverbial is any word, phrase or clause that 'behaves like' an adverb in the sentence, i.e. it modifies the verb, describing how it is carried out, for example:

The chicken crossed the road <u>quickly</u>.	Adverb
The chicken crossed the road <u>in a peculiar manner</u>.	Adverbial phrase
The chicken crossed the road <u>without looking where it was going</u>.	Adverbial clause

All of these adverbials modify the verb *crossed* by describing how the act of crossing the road was carried out. Adverbials can follow on from the main clause, as in all three of the examples above. Alternatively, they can be 'fronted' or placed before the main clause, with a comma between the two parts of the sentence:

<u>Without looking where it was going,</u> the chicken crossed the road.

They can also be embedded within the main clause, with two commas at either side:

The chicken<u>, without looking where it was going,</u> crossed the road.

Adverbials can also indicate the time or place when the action denoted by the verb was carried out:

I played netball with my friends <u>last Saturday</u>.	Adverbial of time
<u>In Britain,</u> tea is usually served with milk.	Adverbial of place

Teaching ideas

Adjectives and adverbs should be introduced in Key Stage 1 and consolidated and developed through Key Stage 2. Before you teach adverbs, make sure that your class have a secure understanding of verbs (for more on verbs, head to Chapter 4).

KS1 ## How am I doing it?

Get all the children in a circle and mime an action such as running. Say to the pupils, 'I am running. But HOW am I running?' The children have to respond with an adverb, e.g. *slowly*, *quickly*, *clumsily*, *heavily*, and then all children mime running in that style. The child who suggested the adverb goes to the middle of the circle and chooses a new action.

KS1 ## Do you ever?

This is a simple, easy-to-resource game for teaching adverbs of frequency. Put a sticky note on each wall of your classroom, each with an adverb of frequency on it. Choose four that cover a range of frequencies, e.g. 'Never, Always, Often, Rarely.' Ask the class to stand in the middle of the classroom and read out a 'do you ever' question, e.g.:

'Do you ever brush your teeth?'

The pupils have to run to the adverb of frequency that best reflects how often they do that particular activity. Here's a list of suggested questions you might like to use:

Do you ever brush your teeth?
Do you ever have playdates after school?
Do you ever eat meat?
Do you ever go on holiday?
Do you ever play in the park?
Do you ever watch TV?
Do you ever go to assembly?
Do you ever do homework?
Do you ever eat vegetables?
Do you ever go to the cinema?

In time you can have the children come up with their own 'do you ever' questions.

KS1 ## The interrogation game

LKS2
UKS2
I use this with Key Stage 1 to teach interrogative adjectives but you could definitely increase the level of challenge and use it with Key Stage 2. Explain that the school mascot has been stolen and we are going to have to work out a list of questions to ask every child in the school as part

of the investigation. Agree on six to eight questions and write them out, drawing attention to the fact that they all begin with an interrogative adjective. Choose a child to be interrogated and two children to be interrogators. The interrogators can ONLY ask the same six to eight questions, in any order, as many times as they want. The aim of the game is for the child being interrogated to keep their story consistent, e.g.:

Interrogator 1:   Where were you yesterday lunchtime?

Child: I was in the playground.

Interrogator 2:   Who were you playing with?

Child: Ben and Grace.

Interrogator 1:   What class are you in?

Child: 2P

Interrogator 2:   Why did you steal the school mascot?

Child: I didn't.

Interrogator 1:   Who did steal the mascot?

Child: I don't know.

Interrogator 1:   Where were you yesterday lunchtime?

Child: I was in the playground.

Interrogator 2:   Who were you playing with?

Child: Jack and Grace.

At this point, the child would lose the game because their story is no longer consistent with their previous answers.

There is an adult version of this game online if you want to play it to get an idea of how it runs: www.kongregate.com/games/brandlibel/indefinite-interrogation-game.

Art critics

This is a good one for art lessons. Introduce the class to a bank of words that could be used to describe a piece of art. (There is an example word bank for you to use on the next page and a printable version of this in the online resources.) Then give each pair a photograph of a famous artwork (or, even better, use their artwork!). In pairs, ask your pupils to introduce the piece of art to their class and give a short description of it. Get the rest of the class to count how many arty adjectives they use. Bonus points for the most original and effective use!

Arty adjectives

Your class can use this word bank to curate their own art exhibitions!

Absorbing	Dynamic	Expressive
Original	Romantic	Abstract
Inspiring	Aesthetically pleasing	Soft
Delicate	Bold	Loud
Atmospheric	Textured	Decorative
Baroque	Avant-garde	Unusual
Awe-inspiring	Conceptual	Reactionary

KS1
LKS2
UKS2

How many adjectives can you find to describe…?

Divide the children into small groups, give each group a noun to modify and set a timer. Challenge them to find as many adjectives as they can to modify that noun. This works well on mini whiteboards. You can add in extra challenges, e.g. 'I will give double marks for quantitative adjectives' or 'You cannot use adjectives to describe the colour.' You can modify this game by choosing more challenging nouns: for Key Stage 1 you might choose a noun such as 'cat', 'ball' or 'bus', whereas you could challenge your Year 5 or 6 pupils to find adjectives to describe a noun like 'peace'.

KS1
LKS2
UKS2

Sing with Grammarsaurus!

Children of all ages will enjoy this (even if your Year 5 and 6 children will only sing along ironically). As you know by now, there is nothing like a song to consolidate an idea to memory. This particular one by Grammarsaurus uses the tune of 'All About That Bass' by Meghan Trainor. All together now, *'It's all about the verb, 'bout the verb…'*. Find it at: www.youtube.com/watch?v=B3hR3BHpeho.

LKS2
UKS2

When to use adjectives

Following the rant in the introduction of this chapter, this is a useful exercise for demonstrating to your pupils how adjectives should be used sparingly. Ask your class to open their reading book to a random page. It can be any book and they don't have to have the same one. Then ask them to count the number of nouns on that page and write it down on a whiteboard. Then ask them to count the number of adjectives and write it down. Without fail, the number of nouns should be far higher than the number of adjectives. Use this as a starting point for a discussion about when and why we use adjectives to maximise their effect.

Reverse simile insults

LKS2

UKS2

Similes are used to compare one thing to another, e.g. 'as hot as the sun' or 'as tired as a teacher at the end of term'. This game requires pupils to use adjectives to create similes where the two things you are comparing are not the same, e.g. 'You've been about as useful as a chocolate teapot.' Once you have established the concept, challenge two pupils to dual using reverse simile insults. The dual continues until one side runs out of ideas, e.g.:

Child 1: 'You are about as clever as a headless chicken.'
Child 2: 'Well, YOU are about as useful as a sunroof in a submarine.'
Child 3: 'And YOU are about as generous as Scrooge before the three ghosts visited him.'

Adverbs of frequency percentages

LKS2

UKS2

Link your maths with your grammar teaching with this percentages activity. Print the cards in the online resources (also shown below), and cut them up so that each table has cards with percentages on and cards with adverbs of frequency on. Explain that 'always' is 100 per cent of the time and 'never' is zero per cent of the time. Challenge pupils to match up the other frequencies with the corresponding percentage. Explain that there is more than one way to do this, so you will be asking them to explain their decisions.

Adverbs of frequency percentage cards

Always	100%
Usually	90%
Frequently	80%
Often	70%
Sometimes	50%
Occasionally	40%
Seldom	30%

Rarely	15%
Never	0%

UKS2 Adverbs and adjectives

This is a challenging game that is probably more suitable for a Year 5 or 6 class. There are some words that can be both adverbs and adjectives, e.g. *slow, tight, hard, fast,* etc. Hand out a set of cards displaying these words (as shown below) to each table. There are printable versions of the cards in the online resources. One child turns over a card at random and then it's a race against time to see which child or pair of children can write two sentences demonstrating how the word can be both an adverb and an adjective.

Adverb and adjective cards

Fast	Late	Just
Half	Clear	Straight
Most	Clean	Low

Chapter 7

Plurals, contractions and apostrophes

Chapter overview

When we asked people to name their most feared grammar demon, apostrophes were named time and time again. In this chapter we will look at:

• The various reasons why some words end in 's'.	**KS1**	Pages 78–79
• The plural forms of words and how to tackle words with irregular plurals.	**LKS2** **UKS2**	Pages 79–82
• The conventions for adding possessive apostrophes to words that already end in 's'.	**LKS2**	Page 82
• The conventions surrounding apostrophes for contraction.	**LKS2**	Pages 82–84
• Ideas and resources to support teaching of these concepts.	**KS1** **LKS2** **UKS2**	Pages 84–88

Ah, apostrophes. Is there anything closer to the smug grammar pedant's heart than the 'correct' deployment of apostrophes? Plurals, contractions and apostrophes, and the various conventions through which the three concepts interact, can cause children (and adults) considerable amounts of confusion. Most primary school teachers will be familiar with the pupil who starts attaching an apostrophe to every word ending in 's' regardless of whether or not it is appropriate. You only need to look at the below-the-line comments on any news website or the replies to any high-profile post on social media to know that if this misconception is not cleared up at school, it doesn't go away on its own.

You may be surprised that we have chosen to include plurals and apostrophes in the same chapter. After all, they are completely different things, and the very mistake that people tend to make is in erroneously associating the two concepts. Hopefully, as you read on, you will realise that there are good reasons why we have done so. This chapter will address some of the real clichés of grammar: *you're* and *your*, *its* and *it's*, and the misuse of apostrophes for pluralised nouns. However, it will also look beyond those clichés and explore why these mistakes remain so prevalent and intractable despite the fact that we talk about them all the time… and how you can cure your pupils of these misconceptions for good.

What you need to know

The letter 's' is something of a menace in English, especially when it appears at the end of a word. Most misunderstandings about apostrophes originate in a lack of understanding of the range of purposes an 's' can have.

The five reasons some English words end in 's'

The reason why so many children and adults struggle with apostrophes and plurals is that a simple point is never made clearly to them: that there are five different reasons why an English word might end in 's' and different conventions apply in each of the five cases. More specifically, two of them require apostrophes and the other three don't. Let's meet them all before tackling some of the issues around them in more detail.

1. **Possession:** Some nouns end in 's' to indicate that they 'possess' the word or words that follow – that, either literally or figuratively, what comes after the noun belongs to the noun. For example:

   Has anyone seen <u>Nandika's</u> pencil case?

   Many of <u>this country's</u> children and adults misuse apostrophes.

   <u>Winter's grip</u> on the countryside was coming to an end.

   Note that a noun that ends in 's' to indicate possession <u>does</u> require an apostrophe.

2. **Contraction:** Some nouns and pronouns end in 's' to indicate the presence of a verb (usually 'is' or 'has') in its contracted (shortened) form. For example:

<u>She's</u> not talking to me at the moment.	*'<u>She's</u>' is a contraction of '<u>She is</u>'.*
<u>David's</u> taken leave of his senses.	*'<u>David's</u>' is a contraction of '<u>David has</u>'.*
<u>Where's</u> she going?	*'<u>Where's</u>' is a contraction of '<u>Where is</u>'.*

   Note that a noun that ends in 's' to indicate contraction also <u>does</u> require an apostrophe.

3. **Plurals:** Some nouns end in 's' to indicate that more than one of that noun is being referred to. For example:

> The <u>swans</u> were swimming on the lake.
>
> I waited an hour for a bus and then three <u>buses</u> turned up at once.
>
> Do you believe in <u>fairies</u>?

Note that a noun that ends in 's' to indicate a plural <u>does not</u> require an apostrophe.

4. **Third-person verbs:** Some verbs end in 's' to indicate that they are in their third person, singular, simple present tense form. (See Chapter 4, 'Types of verb', on page 45 for more about verb tense and person.) For example:

> Blake <u>plays</u> football at breaktime.
>
> My teacher always <u>says</u> we should aim for the stars.
>
> Tan <u>goes</u> to school with his brother.

Note that a verb that ends in 's' to indicate that it is in its third person, singular, simple present tense form also <u>does not</u> require an apostrophe.

5. **It just does!** Some words just end in 's'. Often, but by no means always, they are words we have borrowed or adapted from Latin or Ancient Greek. For example:

> <u>Pericles</u> was <u>famous</u> for his role in the <u>politics</u> of ancient <u>Athens</u>.
>
> <u>James</u> took the <u>bus</u> to the <u>circus</u>.
>
> <u>Mrs Jones</u> studied <u>mathematics</u> at university in <u>Paris</u>.

You'll notice from the examples that words that end in 's' in the singular and non-possessive form <u>do not</u> require an apostrophe.

It is worth taking the time to explore the five reasons why a word can end in 's' with primary pupils. The conventions are pretty simple and most children will be able to get their heads around them eventually. Of course, this approach does require a solid understanding of what nouns and verbs are, which is one of several reasons why the chapters on those two terms are found so early in this book. If you've turned to this chapter because apostrophes, plurals or contractions are the next objective in your English planning, we strongly recommend ensuring that you have given your pupils a solid grounding in nouns and verbs first. Once they have this, understanding the 'five reasons' and learning the basic conventions about apostrophe use becomes pretty easy. However, there are still a number of potential apostrophe catastrophes and plural perils we need to avert!

Irregular plurals

Not all nouns in English have regular plural endings. That is to say, some words cannot be put into their plural form (or *pluralised*) simply by adding 's'. These exceptions are called irregular plurals and they come in several different shapes and sizes. The following table shows you some of the most common examples, but it is not an exhaustive list.

Irregular plural	How to pluralise	Examples
Nouns that end in a 'y' preceded by a consonant in their singular form.	If a noun ends in a 'y' in its singular form, then you need to look at the letter before the 'y' to determine how to pluralise it. If the letter before the 'y' is a vowel (a, e, i, o or u), you simply add an 's' as usual (e.g. *trays*, *toys*, *guys*, *keys*). However, if the letter before the 'y' is a consonant, you remove the 'y' altogether and add the suffix '-ies'.	**My <u>family</u> went on holiday with two other <u>families</u>.** **People from many other <u>countries</u> have visited this <u>country</u>.**
Nouns that end in an 's' preceded by a vowel or another 's' in their singular form.	If a noun ends in an 's' in its singular form, then you need to look at the letter before the 's' to determine how to pluralise it. If the letter before the 's' is a vowel (a, e, i, o or u) or if the word ends in a double 's', then you add 'es'.	**London is well-known for its big red <u>buses</u>.** **The footballer made several great <u>passes</u>.**
Nouns that end in an 's' preceded by a consonant in their singular form.	There aren't many unpluralised nouns that end in a consonant followed by an 's' and, because they are quite rare, they are often mistaken for plurals. However, we do have a few of them in English that derive from Ancient Greek and they include well-known words such as *mathematics*, *politics* and *ethics*. These are all usually uncountable nouns, not plurals. This means that the singular form of a verb would traditionally accompany them.	**<u>Politics is</u> a dirty business.** ~~**Politics are a dirty business.**~~
Nouns that remain unchanged in their plural forms.	There are several words in English that remain unchanged in their plural forms. They are often, but not always, the names of animals. Examples include *fish*, *sheep*, *deer* and *aircraft*.	**The staff were attempting to load 400 <u>deer</u> onto three <u>aircraft</u>.**
Nouns that end in an 'f' or 'fe' preceded by a consonant in their singular form.	If a noun ends in an 'f' or 'fe' in its singular form, then you need to look at the letter before the 'f' to determine how to pluralise it. If the letter before the 'f' is a vowel or if the word ends in double 'f' then you usually just add 's'. However, there are exceptions to this (*thief* and *thieves*, for example). If the letter before the 'f' is a consonant other than 'f', you almost always remove the 'f' and replace it with the suffix '-ves', e.g.: **calf – calves** **knife – knives** **wharf – wharves** **self – selves** **life – lives**	**We should all take the time to reflect on our own <u>lives</u> and strive to improve <u>ourselves</u>.**

Some nouns that contain a double 'o'.	Some nouns that contain a double 'o' are pluralised by turning 'oo' into 'ee', e.g.: **foot – feet** **goose – geese** **tooth – teeth** Unfortunately, just as many nouns containing a double 'o' don't conform to this pattern at all and are pluralised by adding 's' in the usual way: **book – books** **hoop – hoops** **noose – nooses** We wish that we could say there was a trick to telling which is which but children just have to learn them!	<u>**Geese**</u> **do not have** <u>**teeth**</u>**.**
Nouns ending in 'o'.	Some words that end in 'o' are pluralised by adding 'es', some are pluralised by adding 's' as usual, and for some both options are equally valid. Here are some examples: **tomato – tomatoes** **radio – radios** **avocado – avocados** **mango – mangos/mangoes** **volcano – volcanos/volcanoes** The 'es' suffix is more likely to be applied to words where the 'o' is preceded by a consonant and less likely if the 'o' is preceded by a vowel, but these are by no means universal rules.	**The greengrocer sold** <u>**tomatoes**</u>**,** <u>**avocados**</u> **and** <u>**mangoes**</u>**.** Or **The greengrocer sold** <u>**tomatoes**</u>**,** <u>**avocados**</u> **and** <u>**mangos**</u>**.**
Latin plurals.	Some words that came to Britain from the Romans are pluralised using Latin grammar rules. There are hundreds of these, especially in science and mathematics. Some well-known examples are: **antenna – antennae** **formula – formulae** **index – indices** **vertex – vertices** **criterion – criteria** **analysis – analyses** **basis – bases** **axis – axes** **appendix – appendices** **bacterium – bacteria** **fungus – fungi**	**A cube has eight** <u>**vertices**</u>**.** **Make sure you label both** <u>**axes**</u> **on your graph.**

| Completely irregular exceptions. | Some nouns have plural forms that don't conform to any sort of rule at all. Unfortunately, this includes some nouns we use very regularly, e.g.:

man – men
child – children
mouse – mice | **The <u>children</u> crept past as quietly as <u>mice</u>.** |

How does the possessive apostrophe work if a word already ends in 's'?

Sometimes a noun already ends in 's' and the writer wishes to indicate that something belongs to it with an apostrophe. If the noun already ends in an 's' because it is a plural, you should simply add an apostrophe after the 's' but do not add an additional 's'. For example:

The storm was sent by Zeus and Poseidon. It was the gods' vengeance.
The football boots belong to the ladies. They are the ladies' football boots.
Many thieves hid there. It was the thieves' hide-out.

If adding a possessive apostrophe to an irregular plural that doesn't end in 's', you add an 's' afterwards, as you would if the noun was singular. For example:

The geese's nest was located on a quiet island.
It is inadvisable to dismiss children's opinions out of hand.

If adding a possessive apostrophe to a singular noun that ends in 's' regardless of the situation, you have two choices:

1. Add the apostrophe and an additional 's', e.g.:

   James's school uniform was too small.

   Charles Dickens's novel, *Oliver Twist*, was written in 1837.

2. Add an apostrophe to the end of the word, e.g.:

   Louis' trumpet needs tuning.

   The Eiffel Tower is one of Paris' main tourist attractions.

More about contractions

The important point to make to children about contractions is that the apostrophe usually replaces the missing letters of the word that has been shortened. Here are some of the most common examples:

1. The apostrophe sometimes replaces the *i* from the word *is*:

   He's not joking.

   I think Laura's regretting her decision.

2. The apostrophe sometimes replaces the *h* and the *a* from the word *have*:

   I've forgotten my glasses.

   They've been doing this for a long time.

3. The apostrophe sometimes replaces the *o* from the word *not*:

   I don't believe it.

   We mustn't talk about this.

4. The apostrophe sometimes replaces the first four letters of the word *would*:

   You'd have arrived by now if you'd taken the bus.

   They'd make a different decision if they knew all the facts.

5. The apostrophe sometimes replaces the *w* and the *i* from the word *will*:

   We'll be fine.

   They'll just have to find another solution.

6. The apostrophe sometimes replaces the *a* from the word *are*:

   You're absolutely right.

   We're bringing dessert.

There are also a couple of irregular contractions you will need to make your pupils aware of, most notably *won't* (will not) and *can't* (cannot). The latter of these is especially important as when some children, especially those with particular regional accents, attempt to spell it phonetically, the consequences can be most unfortunate!

You're and your, they're and their, it's and its

These three pairs of homophones should always be taught together, as the distinction between them is exactly the same. *You're*, *they're* and *it's* are all contractions formed by combining a personal pronoun with a simple present tense form of the verb *to be*:

I hope you're coming to my party – I hope you are coming to my party.
They're not listening to me – They are not listening to me.
It's getting late – It is getting late.

Your, *their* and *its* are all possessive adjectives, indicating whom something belongs to:

I think this is <u>your</u> pen.
<u>Their</u> house is rather untidy.
This school really cares about <u>its</u> pupils.

Teaching these spelling differences as a set helps to reinforce the pattern and makes it much easier for children to remember. Obviously, it still leaves you with a third *there* to address (and potentially *yore* if you really want to go there!). However, it's particularly helpful for dealing with the understandable confusion that children have about *it's* and *its*. Consider this sentence:

The robot removed <u>its</u> arm in order to repair it.

A child who has understood everything in this chapter might quite reasonably look at this sentence, go back to the 'Five reasons' and conclude that the arm belongs to the robot, therefore it is possessive, and place an apostrophe in the word *its*. Teaching the its/it's distinction alongside the your/you're distinction and the their/they're distinction makes it much easier for children to see the pattern. The point can be reinforced even more effectively by changing the word *its* in the above sentence to *his*:

The robot removed <u>his</u> arm in order to repair it.

It will be obvious to most children that *his* does not require an apostrophe and you can explain that *its* is a possessive adjective equivalent to *his* (neither requiring an apostrophe), whereas *it's* is a contracted subject and verb equivalent to *he's* (both requiring an apostrophe).

Teaching ideas

Just a little heads-up – some of these Key Stage 1 teaching ideas are better suited to Year 2 rather than Year 1. The 2014 National Curriculum states that apostrophes for omission and possession are only to be taught from Year 2 onwards, whereas plural noun suffixes -*s* and -*es* are to be taught from Year 1. As always, you are the expert on your class, so just use your judgement and adapt things to make them work for the children in your lessons.

KS1 ## Sticky note suffixes

Choose 15 singular words and write them on sticky notes. Make enough to give one to half of the children in the class. Then give the other half of the class a sticky note with either the -*es* or the -*s* suffix written on it. Then, in total silence, the class have to go round finding an appropriate partner to make their word plural. Once they have found one another, the pairs are allowed to talk and explain to the class how they knew to choose that person, e.g. *'My word was fox so I chose someone with the -es suffix because if the word ends with ch, sh, s, x or z, you use -es to make it plural.'* For children who are still learning to decode, you might want to include a picture of the noun. You can increase the challenge in this activity by including more irregular plural suffixes, e.g. -*oes* or -*ves*. If you want to, you can build in cross-curricular links by choosing words linked to your science, geography or history topic, e.g. 'volcano' (for which the suffix would be -*s* or -*es*).

Put in the apostrophes: Key Stage 1

KS1

Use the Key Stage 1 modelled writing below (there is a printable version in the online resources). Read through the text as a class, then in pairs ask pupils to put in the ten missing apostrophes for omission and possession. Choose one pair to come and talk through their answers. The modelled writing in this book is linked to the Great Fire of London (because there are so many uncertainties in this world, but the one thing you can be damn sure of is that Year 2 will learn about the Great Fire of London). You could build cross-curricular links by creating your own modelled text based on your own topic.

Key Stage 1 modelled writing

Samuel Pepys Life

Samuel Pepys lived from 1633 to 1703. He is famous because he wrote a diary that covered two important events in Englands history: the Great Plague in 1665 and the Great Fire of London in 1666. Pepys diary gives a fascinating, first-hand account of the fire spreading from the Kings bakers house and across the city. He even writes about burying his cheese and wine, as he didnt want them destroyed by the fire! Despite all the destruction caused by the fire, Pepys house, office and diary survived in one piece. Pepys didnt write his diary for other people to read. In fact he wrote it in a sort of secret code called shorthand. It wasnt published until 1825 and its helped us understand more about what life was like in London in the 17th century.

Plural catch

KS1

Use your PE lessons to reinforce some grammar! Have the class stand in a circle. Start by throwing a ball to a child and saying, 'The word is _____.' The child then has to say, 'The plural is spelt _____' before throwing it back to you. For example:

Teacher: The word is frog.
(Throws ball to pupil.)

Pupil: The plural is spelt: f-r-o-g-s.
(Throws ball back to the teacher.)

Repeat the game, differentiating the level of challenge to suit each child's ability. What I like about this activity is that all the children will get to hear the correct spelling said aloud so they are involved, even if it isn't their turn to throw or catch the ball. Once your class are more confident with this game, you can adapt the rules so they don't have to throw the ball back to you each time but can instead choose a new word before throwing it to someone else in the class. It also helps reinforce spelling – you could choose words linked to the topic you are studying or words that include the spelling convention you are learning. The possibilities are endless!

Plural bingo

This activity would be best suited to upper Key Stage 1 or lower Key Stage 2. Edit and print out copies of the bingo board in the online resources (also shown below for reference). Give a slightly different version to each pair of pupils. Instead of calling out numbers or words, in plural bingo you call out a rule, e.g. 'a word that is identical in both the singular and the plural forms' or 'a word that becomes plural by changing the vowels'. Pupils have to cross off the word they have that applies to that rule. Three in a row and they can shout, 'Bingo!' but they then have to explain how each word they have crossed off satisfies the rule that was read out. You can increase the level of challenge by asking the children to draw their own three-by-three grid and choose their own range of singular nouns to put on the board.

Bingo board

woman	sheep	potato
orange	pencil	knife
child	watch	shrimp

 Animal life cycles

Animal life cycles is a topic taught in both Key Stage 1 and Key Stage 2 science. There are plenty of opportunities within this topic to consolidate your work on plurals. Animal names are particularly interesting – have a look at how they change when they are singular and plural. Most of the words that stay the same when they are singular and plural are animal names, e.g. *sheep, shrimp, deer, fish,* etc. Then have a look at the names for the infant animals and discuss how they change, e.g. puppy becomes *puppies* and calf becomes *calves.*

 Why is there an apostrophe in o'clock?

O'clock is a common spelling error, so teach it in your maths lesson on time. Explain that an apostrophe is used in o'clock because it is a contraction of the phrase 'of the clock'. As with the other contractions, the apostrophe takes the place of missing words and letters. There is no game or specific activity we are suggesting for this; just use the opportunity to develop your class's spelling in subjects other than English!

Beat the clock: an apostrophes game

In this activity, pupils have to convert words into their contracted forms:

Should have

Would have

Must have

Shall not

Should not

Will not

Write them up on the board and set a timer on the board for 20 seconds. You can vary the level of challenge by increasing or decreasing the time or choosing simpler contractions, e.g. *do not*, or more complex ones, e.g. *dare not*. Challenge your pupils to write the contracted versions on a mini whiteboard before the timer runs out. First pair to complete all contractions wins!

Put in the apostrophes: Key Stage 2

Use the Key Stage 2 modelled writing below (there is a printable version in the online resources). Read through the text as a class and then get pupils to put in the missing apostrophes for omission and possession. You can adjust the level of challenge by asking your class to work in pairs or individually. Choose one child or pair of children to come and talk through the answers. The one that is likely to catch pupils out is the sentence, 'Her bedroom door creaked on its hinges.' When they are first learning about apostrophes, it is common for children to put them in 'its', so use this activity as a chance to discuss why, in this context, 'its' does not need an apostrophe.

Key Stage 2 modelled writing

'Rise and shine, sleepy head! Its time to get up!' called Emilys mum through the crack in her bedroom door. Emilys eyes felt heavy. She decided it was best to pretend she hadnt heard her mums wake-up call and turned over to go back to sleep.

Just as she was drifting off, she heard her brother James footsteps pattering down the hall. Emily groaned. She wasnt in the mood to see her annoying little brother. James footsteps got louder and louder and then suddenly they stopped. Her bedroom door creaked on its hinges as he gently pushed it open.

'Emily! Are you awake yet? Mum said its time to get up. Were going to be late for school if you dont get up now.'

Emily groaned loudly as she slowly sat up. She knew she couldnt put it off any longer: it was time to get up.

Complete the plurals table

This is a straightforward and simple activity to assess your class's knowledge of plurals. Print out and laminate copies of the below table from the online resources (that way you can use it repeatedly). Give a copy to each pupil and give them five minutes to complete it with examples of each plural. Once again, you can increase the challenge by reducing the time!

+ -s	+ -es	Change y to i + -es	Change f to v + -es	Singular same as plural	Latin plurals	'oo' to 'ee'	Completely irregular

Chapter 8

Punctuation at the end of a sentence

Chapter overview

This is a very important chapter. Why? It's about punctuation at the end of the sentence! Read on to find out more about full stops, question marks, exclamation marks and ellipses... In this chapter we will look at:

• How to use full stops, question marks, exclamation marks and ellipses to end sentences.	KS1	Pages 90–92
• How to combine question marks, exclamation marks and ellipses where appropriate.	LKS2	Page 92
• Ideas and resources to support teaching of these concepts.	KS1 LKS2 UKS2	Pages 93–94

All good things must come to an end. Once we've written a sentence we must be able to end it, and this will usually involve one (or possibly more) of four punctuation marks: the full stop, the question mark, the exclamation mark and the ellipsis. In this chapter we will explore each of these options in more detail and consider some of the implications that these choices can have on our pupils' writing.

What you need to know

As we have already established, the simplest way to make sense when writing in English is to express our ideas in sentences that contain, as a minimum, a subject and a verb phrase. There are countless types of sentence that we can write and countless different effects we can generate. The effect we wish to create informs the choice of punctuation mark we make at the end.

Full stops

Typically, of course, a sentence ends with a full stop (or a 'period' as you will sometimes hear it called in American English). Sometimes, the presence of a full stop might indicate a good place for someone reading aloud to pause, but not always. A lot of teachers have tried to talk about 'pauses' in an effort to explain where full stops should go in a child's writing. This can be misleading and counterproductive. It is clearer and more helpful to ensure that your children can identify the subject(s) and verb phrase(s) in every sentence they write so that it becomes crystal clear where one sentence ends and another begins (see Chapter 5, 'Subject, verb and object', page 55).

Question marks

As well as adorning the costumes of several past incarnations of *Doctor Who*, question marks replace full stops at the end of interrogative sentences – a posh word for 'questions'. Sometimes, especially in older grammar reference materials, question marks are called 'interrogative marks'. Some children often need to be reminded to include question marks and they also need to be reminded that some interrogative sentences can be quite subtle:

I assume everything is OK?
That's not a good idea, is it?
Dr Livingstone, I presume?

As these examples show, the boundary between what is and what isn't a question isn't always clear. All of the sentences above could be ended with different punctuation marks but it would change their meanings in rather nuanced ways. Consider:

I assume everything is OK…
That's not a good idea, is it!
Dr Livingstone, I presume.

We can't say for sure which set of sentences is more 'correct' without knowing the context in which the words are said, or indeed the intonation with which they are intended to be read aloud. Heightening the pitch of your voice at the end of a sentence in English tends to indicate that you are asking a question – unless of course you're a gap-year student who does it every time you utter a sentence of any kind. However, whenever the primary purpose of the sentence is to ask your audience a question, either literally or rhetorically, a question mark would be the preferable punctuation mark with which to conclude it.

Exclamation marks

Many children overuse exclamation marks! They put them at the end of sentences that are neither funny nor surprising nor emphatic! They think it makes their writing more interesting!

Annoying, isn't it? It's also quite unsurprising when you look at the way in which magazines and web content intended for children are often presented. Exclamation marks abound. Perhaps, then, the most important point to make about exclamation marks is that they shouldn't be overused. They tend to indicate statements that are amusing or unexpected or, when included in direct speech, they may indicate that the manner in which a character says something is louder or more emphatic than usual. If you use them too often then they *become* usual and their whole purpose is negated.

There has been a certain amount of heated discussion about the Department for Education's definition of an <u>exclamation sentence</u>, which forms part of the National Curriculum and appears to have been invented as a concept in the last few years for the purposes of writing assessment. The Standards and Testing Agency (2016) explains what is meant by an exclamation sentence as follows:

> *'The national curriculum states that an exclamation is one of the four forms of sentences. An exclamation must be introduced by a phrase with "what" or "how" and should be followed by a subject + verb + any other elements. It is typically demarcated by an exclamation mark, for example:*
>
> *What big teeth you have, Grandma!*
>
> *How beautiful Cinderella looks in that dress!*
>
> *The definition of an exclamation should not be confused with the uses of the exclamation mark for punctuation. The exclamation mark can be used in a variety of sentence forms and not just in exclamations.*
>
> *Pupils at KS1 who are "working at the expected" and/or "working at greater depth" standards must use sentences with different forms in their writing.'*

It's a very strange state of affairs, but Key Stage 1 and Key Stage 2 writing assessment guidance requires children to be able to write sentences in a 'range of forms' and this is one of the few that is explicitly mentioned. Therefore, for as long as this assessment regime persists, it is probably something you will want to teach your pupils. We have no opinion on the extent to which sentences like this constitute 'good writing'.

Ellipses

Ellipses is the plural of ellipsis. Let's deal with that straightaway! An ellipsis is understood by most teachers as what the man or woman in the street would call 'dot dot dot'. However, the word ellipsis actually refers to any situation in which words are omitted that the reader is expected to be able to understand from contextual clues. For example:

Look out! Tiger!

This utterance consists of an imperative (the command to 'look out') and a single word. Reading it, you will interpret the use of a single noun 'tiger' to stand for a longer and much more urgent statement, such as 'There is a tiger over there.' The rest of the words have been omitted but are (literally) taken as read by the reader. Even though there are no triplicated dots to be seen, this is actually an example of the grammatical concept of ellipsis.

However, the form of ellipsis most of us are more familiar with is that which occurs at the end of a sentence. When the author wishes to highlight for the reader that something important has been left unsaid or unresolved or that there is some extra meaning that the reader is intended to infer, this might be signposted with a series of (usually three) dots:

Mr Layburn hoped that now, at long last, he would finally have some peace and quiet…

The ellipsis here is telling us that there is more to be said about the statement than what is literally written on the page. Most likely, in a case such as this, we can infer that Mr Layburn did not in fact get to enjoy the peace and quiet and that something would come along and shatter it.

This sort of ellipsis can also be used to indicate interruptions or incomplete sentences:

'Ladies and gentlemen, thank you for coming today and thank you for…'

This gives us an immediate sense of someone who has stopped speaking mid-sentence. Perhaps they have forgotten what they were going to say or noticed someone in their audience whom they're shocked to see. There are many different ways in which ellipsis punctuation can be used and it's almost always a stylistic choice. Like the exclamation mark, children should be encouraged to experiment with it but eventually discouraged from overusing it.

Combining punctuation marks

Sometimes two or more punctuation marks can be combined to end a sentence. Consider these examples:

We're going on holiday tomorrow!!!
But if you didn't do it and I didn't do it then who…?
What on Earth are you talking about?!

The basic ideas behind these punctuation choices are clear. The triplicated exclamation marks in the first sentence indicate the writer's extreme level of excitement at the prospect of going on holiday. In the second sentence, a question has been posed but some of the words have been left unsaid, thus the writer has opted to use both an ellipsis and a question mark. In the third sentence, a rhetorical question has been posed but the question mark has been combined with an exclamation mark in order to indicate the writer's incredulity or amazement at whatever has been said to prompt this response. This particular combination is sometimes referred to as an 'interrobang'. There are no hard and fast rules about these combinations and they tend to be a matter of stylistic choice, although writing in which question marks and exclamation marks constantly appear in large clusters can be profoundly annoying for the reader. Generally speaking, a question mark and an exclamation mark would follow and not precede an ellipsis and a full stop wouldn't usually be combined with any of the other punctuation marks. Other than that, the writer is free to use and combine these punctuation marks however they see fit. Once you are confident that your pupils have understood the different types of punctuation and their purpose, you can encourage them to play around with these combinations in their writing.

Teaching ideas

When teaching punctuation at the end of a sentence to Key Stage 1, your priority should be identifying where the full stops go and understanding that there are different types of sentence, e.g. statement, question, command, etc.

Add in the punctuation

KS1

This is a very simple activity to consolidate your pupils' understanding of different sentence types. Provide them with a range of sentences (you can use the examples below if you wish – there is a printable worksheet with these examples in the online resources) and get them to add either a full stop, a question mark or an exclamation mark. Once they've punctuated all the sentences, encourage them to read them aloud, adjusting their tone to match the punctuation marks. If you want to build in a cross-curricular link, you can give your pupils sentences about their geography or history topic.

Example sentences

Does your mum work in an office
Whose jumper is this
I live on Bellevue Road in Barnet
Stop it
Soon it will be my birthday
Look out
Who else likes chocolate
Has anyone seen my book bag
We are going on holiday to Thailand
What a mean thing to say
A rhinoceros horn is made of hair
What a beautiful day
We need to buy more butter if we want to bake a cake

Sing the sentence song

KS1

This catchy little tune will reinforce your teaching and revises the key facts about the different types of sentence. Sing it together as a class: www.youtube.com/watch?v=0Wrv_ZviMEc.

Statement/question/exclamation

KS1

LKS2

UKS2

This is a good way to highlight how punctuation can change the meaning of the sentence. Give your pupils a sentence to copy down without any sentence punctuation, e.g.:

You are in danger

Then ask them to write it as a statement, a question and an exclamation, as follows:

You are in danger. You are in danger? You are in danger!

This will probably lead to a discussion about how punctuation changes the meaning and purpose of the sentence. You could even get your class to role-play using the different sentences and come up with scenarios to fit them.

Model it

In case you haven't already clocked this, we are big fans of modelled writing. It is particularly effective when teaching sentence punctuation, as you can model your thought process as a writer, e.g. 'OK, so I have written: "The fox is eating out of the bin." Is this an independent clause? Does it make sense on its own? Does it have a subject, verb and object? So, we can agree this is a sentence and it needs some punctuation.' It's important for the pupils to see the writing process, so model as often as possible.

Add in the punctuation

This is a step up from the Key Stage 1 activity (which you might want to use with a lower Key Stage 2 class). Give your class an extract of text without any sentence punctuation (there is one provided below and a printable version of this in the online resources) and ask them to add it in. Once they're happy with it, get them to compare their work with a partner. It is likely that they will have punctuated the text slightly differently; discuss how their punctuation choices have changed the text and which they prefer.

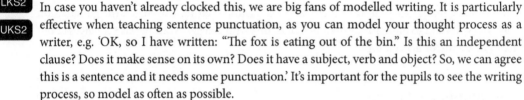

Extract

Monday was the first day of the summer holidays my mum woke me up really early because we had to get to the airport we took the train to Gatwick and checked in our bags then we had breakfast in a cafe and I had a croissant and some orange juice after what felt like hours of waiting it was time to board I was so excited there were TVs in the back of the seats can you believe it I watched two films *Cats & Dogs 2* and *Toy Story 4* the flight to Thailand took quite a long time we got given lunch on a special tray like at school how are your holidays going are you going anywhere nice I wonder what we are going to do tomorrow

Part Two

Extending sentences

Chapter 9

Main and subordinate clauses

Chapter overview

In this chapter we will defeat another common grammar demon: clauses (and not the friendly Mr and Mrs who live in the North Pole kind). In this chapter we will look at:

• The differences between main and subordinate clauses.	LKS2	Pages 98–99
• The conventions for linking more than one main clause.	LKS2	Pages 99–100
• The conventions for linking main and subordinate clauses.	LKS2	Page 100
• Ideas and resources to support teaching of these concepts.	KS1 LKS2 UKS2	Pages 100–102

The first section of this book covered the basics of making sense in English: writing words and constructing simple sentences. This section deals with the way in which simple sentences can be combined and modified in order to make more complex grammatical constructions. In this chapter, we will be exploring clauses. Generally speaking, any attempt to introduce the concept of a clause to a group of primary children will need to start with some sort of joke or pun about Santa Claus. If you don't go there first, your pupils will invariably lead you there themselves. With that formality out of the way, you can dive into the differences between a main clause and a subordinate clause. What's a subordinate clause? One of Santa's elves, obviously.

What you need to know

Our teachers barely mentioned clauses when we were at primary school – the likelihood is that your own experience was similar. It's easy to dismiss ideas we weren't taught ourselves as unnecessary or superfluous. In this case, we think that would be a mistake. There are large parts of the English curriculum that become much easier to teach once children have a secure understanding of clauses.

Main clauses

Throughout most of the first part of this book, we explored simple sentences. These are sentences that contain only one <u>clause</u> or, more specifically, a <u>main clause</u>. A clause is a grammatical construction that expresses meaning: it describes a relationship, a circumstance or a state of affairs. It always includes a verb or a verb phrase and it usually includes a subject too (although it can be an implied subject or a dummy subject – see Appendix 6, page 191). Consider this example:

<u>The boy went to the cinema</u>.

This sentence is made of one clause that tells us what the boy did. This is a simple sentence (see Chapter 5, 'Subject, verb and object', page 55, for more about simple sentences). Any sentence containing more than one clause can be described as a <u>complex sentence</u>.

<u>The boy went to the cinema</u> and <u>the girl went swimming</u>.

This sentence is made of two clauses. It tells us both what the boy did and what the girl did. In this case, both clauses are of equal importance to the meaning of the sentence and they are separated by the word *and*, which is acting as a <u>coordinating conjunction</u> (see Chapter 11, 'Prepositions and conjunctions', page 111). Both clauses have equal importance and both would *make sense on their own* (as demonstrated in the first example: 'The boy went to the cinema.'). We would therefore say that this sentence is made of two main clauses. This type of complex sentence can also be known as a compound sentence, as it looks like two sentences merged together. The two main clauses can be connected by a coordinating conjunction ('and' in the example above) or by a semi-colon:

<u>The boy went to the cinema</u>; <u>the girl went swimming</u>.

There are also some situations in which two main clauses could be separated by a colon (see Chapter 14, page 135, for more on semi-colons and colons). However, it is not acceptable in English grammar to separate two main clauses with a comma. This is called 'comma splicing' and it's a common mistake among both children and adults:

~~**The boy went to the cinema, the girl went swimming.**~~

Here are some more examples of sentences containing two main clauses:

I <u>love her</u>; <u>she loves me</u>.
<u>There was only one way we could win</u>: <u>we would have to unite and use all our different abilities</u>.
<u>I want to learn</u> so <u>I work hard at school</u>.

These examples demonstrate the three most common ways of joining two main clauses without starting a new sentence: using a semi-colon, using a colon and using a coordinating conjunction. Coordinating conjunctions tend to be those words that you were taught 'can't go at the start of a sentence' like *and* or *but*. This is not always the case, but the set of coordinating conjunctions is generally accepted as including the following seven words: *and, but, for, nor, or, so* and *yet*.

Subordinate clauses

Now consider this complex sentence:

<u>**The boy went to the cinema** **because he was bored.**</u>

This sentence is also made of two clauses. It tells us what the boy did and it tells us why. Notice, however, that in this example, the two clauses are not of equal importance to the meaning of the sentence. The second clause is introduced by the word *because*, which is acting as a <u>subordinating conjunction</u> (see Chapter 11, 'Prepositions and conjunctions', page 111). The first clause is grammatically more important and the second only really makes sense because of the first. We therefore say that this sentence is composed of a main clause and a subordinate clause. You will often find that sentences like this can be rearranged so that the subordinate clause appears before (or even embedded within) the main clause. For example:

<u>**Because he was bored,** **the boy went to the cinema.**</u>

Notice that when the subordinate clause is <u>fronted</u> in this way, we tend to separate it from the main clause with a comma. Here are several other sentences containing a main and a subordinate clause. The subordinate clause has been underlined in each one:

The detective searched the office, <u>hoping he'd find some useful clues.</u>
<u>When she had finished her homework,</u> Selin went to play outside.
The puppy, <u>whose name was Nelly,</u> ran excitedly into the garden.

There are several different types of subordinate clause included in these examples and we'll be exploring some of them in more detail in the next chapter – 'Types of subordinate clause'. You will notice that, unlike two main clauses, a main and a subordinate clause can be separated with a comma. You will also notice in the examples above that there are three places you might find the subordinate clause. It might <u>follow on</u> from the main clause and appear after it, it might be <u>fronted</u> and appear before the main clause, or it might be <u>embedded</u> in the middle of the main clause, marked out with two commas either side. An embedded clause will usually be found immediately after the subject of the main clause but it can sometimes be found after the object too.

Greater complexity

Sentences can include any number of main and subordinate clauses, so long as they are linked together in a grammatically acceptable way. Consider this very complex sentence:

Despite <u>the pain he felt in his thigh</u> and <u>despite the doubts in his mind</u>, <u>he kept on running</u>, <u>hoping he could catch up with his opponent</u>; <u>his calves burned</u> and <u>his muscles ached but Ben</u>, <u>who had never lost a race</u>, <u>was determined to succeed.</u>

This sentence consists of eight clauses: four main clauses and four subordinate clauses. We often talk to children about writing a 'range of sentences', including 'shorter, simpler sentences' and 'longer, more complex ones'. There are two points we need to make here. The first is that, grammatically speaking, simple sentences are not necessarily short and complex sentences are not necessarily long. Secondly, if children are genuinely going to understand what we are asking them to do when we ask them to vary their sentence structures, we need to be talking to them about clauses and we need to be doing it fairly early on. If it were up to us, children would be introduced to clauses in Key Stage 1 as they are very much the building blocks of sentences.

Dependence and independence

Throughout this book, we use the language of the National Curriculum to talk about clauses and have therefore stuck to the terms 'main clause' and 'subordinate clause' in this chapter. However, it is worth being aware that both these grammatical constructions go by another name: a main clause is also known as an <u>independent clause</u> and a subordinate clause is also known as a <u>dependent clause</u>. These can be quite helpful terms to share with children, partly because they are terms they may encounter elsewhere but also because they give them a clearer idea about what the two concepts actually mean. A main clause is independent – it is meaningful and relevant even if you take the other clauses away. A subordinate clause, by contrast, is dependent. It depends on the main clause for meaning and relevance.

Teaching ideas

There are just a few suggested activities for teaching in this chapter because when we think about how we actually teach this topic, we don't use songs, art or cross-curricular links but we just give pupils lots of opportunities to identify and add clauses. If you are looking for more activities on different types of subordinate clause then head over to Chapter 10, page 103. The priority at this point is making sure that your pupils understand the difference between a main clause and a subordinate clause. The Department for Education has put clauses in Year 3, but in Year 2 children need to learn about subordinating and coordinating conjunctions, which, in our opinion, you cannot teach without first teaching children about clauses.

  ## Identify the main clause

We would argue that main clauses can be taught from Year 2 onwards and an activity like this is a good place to start. Once you have explained the difference between a main clause and a subordinate clause, give your pupils a variety of sentences and ask them to identify the main clause. Encourage them to explain how they know they have found the main clause. There are a few sentences you can use for this activity on the next page, which are also available as a printable worksheet in the online resources. You can do this activity with older pupils but you might want to increase the challenge by getting them to identify main clauses in their reading books rather than in individual sentences. Alternatively, you can use the modelled text on page 102, which is also available as a worksheet online.

Example sentences

Having finished her coffee, Mrs Paramour left for work.

Feeling tired and cold, the children climbed into bed.

The cat, who had just been fed, was hungry.

Although she knew it was wrong, Rebecca stole her brother's snack.

After the heatwave had subsided, the grass in the meadow turned brown.

Most people drive cars, although they are bad for the environment.

Mr French bought the paper when he was on the train.

Add the main clause

`KS1` `LKS2`

Once you are confident that your class can identify a main clause in a sentence, you can move on to getting them to add a main clause. For this activity, you need to provide your pupils with a subordinate clause and get them to write their own main clause. For Key Stage 1 pupils, you might want to just get them to add a main clause to the end of the subordinate clause, but you could increase the challenge for Key Stage 2 by asking them to vary where in the sentence they put the subordinate clause. What you want to focus on here is an understanding that a main clause could form a sentence on its own AND that the main clause has to link with the subordinate clause. Once again, you can use the subordinate clauses below, which are also available as a printable worksheet in the online resources for this activity.

Example subordinate clauses

Despite the fact the sign told them not to,

Although he did not want to,

When I grow up,

Because it was cold,

Having finished all her chores,

As the sun went down,

Having eaten her lunch,

Without wishing to seem rude,

Say a sentence

`LKS2` `UKS2`

Sit the class in a circle and ask the first children to say either a main clause or a subordinate clause, e.g. 'the cat sat on the mat'. The next child must then say a subordinate clause (in this case) to complete the sentence, e.g. 'because he was tired'. The rest of the circle can give a thumbs up or a thumbs down depending on whether they think the clauses create a sentence.

 ## Modelled text

 Give your class a copy of the following text and get them to identify the main and subordinate clauses. There is a printable version of the text available as a worksheet in the online resources. From there you could move on to a lesson about the different types of subordinate clause and the role they play in the sentence. For more information on subordinate clause, head to Chapter 10, page 103. You could also use this modelled text in a creative writing lesson and challenge your class to continue the story (using their new and improved knowledge of clauses!).

Text

As quickly as they could, the children shuffled into the school hall. The headteacher, who was usually a stern figure, looked uncharacteristically relaxed. The children glanced at one another, unsure as to why they were there. Assembly was normally at nine o'clock but this one had been called at half past two in the afternoon. What was going on? Whatever it was, something did not feel right. When everyone was seated, Mrs Li shut the doors. The teachers were seated on either side of the hall, shuffling nervously in their seats. The ticking of the clock was deafening. After what felt like an eternity, the headteacher spoke.

'Good morning, everyone! I have gathered you into the hall because I have some marvellous news to share...'

Chapter 10

Types of subordinate clause

Chapter overview

Continuing with the battle of the clauses, this chapter is all about how to use clauses to extend sentences and add more detail. We will be looking at:

• How to extend sentences using relative clauses.	**LKS2**	Pages 104–105
• Identifying and using adverbial and participle clauses.	**UKS2**	Pages 105–106
• Exploring other types of subordinate clause such as interrogative and comment clauses.	**UKS2**	Pages 106–107
• Ideas and resources to support teaching of these concepts.	**LKS2** **UKS2**	Pages 107–110

Once your pupils can identify the difference between a main clause and a subordinate clause, the next step is to understand and use a variety of different subordinate clauses. Subordinate clauses take many different forms and serve many different functions in sentences. It's no bad thing for children to know the names of different types of subordinate clause, but even more important is that they understand the effect that different types of subordinate clause have on the way in which their reader will interpret their writing.

What you need to know

It would be impossible to list every type of subordinate clause in this chapter, so we will explore some of the most common variations that you might want to encourage your pupils to try to include in their own writing.

Relative clauses

This is the only type of subordinate clause that the National Curriculum and the Year 6 grammar, punctuation and spelling test require children to be able to name. Relative clauses (also known as adjectival clauses) are a form of <u>parenthesis</u>: they give the reader more information about the people or events referred to in the main clause. They often begin with, or at least contain, a relative pronoun such as *who, whose, which, that* or *when*. They are usually found either following on from the main clause or embedded within it using two commas. Here are some examples in which the relative clause has been underlined.

Example 1

Sarah had a little dog, <u>which she adored</u>.

In this sentence, the relative clause follows on after the main clause. It starts with the relative pronoun *which* and gives the reader more information about the object of the main clause: the little dog.

Example 2

Andy, <u>whose appetite was legendary</u>, always went back for seconds.

In this sentence, the relative clause has been embedded within the main clause with two commas. It starts with the relative pronoun *whose* and gives the reader more information about the subject of the main clause: Andy.

Example 3

She went to see her father, <u>the only person who would be able to help</u>.

Notice that in this example, the relative pronoun *who* is not actually at the start of the relative clause but in the middle of it. However, the function of the clause is to provide the reader with more information about the object of the main clause: her father.

Examples 4 and 5

After staring at his phone nervously for some time, Jack finally decided to ring the girl <u>he'd met at the party</u>.

In this example, the relative pronoun *who* has been omitted altogether. It could be placed between *girl* and *he'd* but in this instance it isn't necessary for the sentence to be grammatically acceptable. Sometimes, a relative clause is 'demoted' to being a mere phrase by omitting both the relative pronoun and the verb. In the following example, the relative pronoun *which* and the verb *was* have been omitted:

In 1945, <u>a year of dramatic change all over Europe</u>, Winston Churchill was replaced as prime minister by Clement Attlee.

In this example, the underlined section serves as a <u>noun phrase</u>. If the author had chosen to write '*which was* a year of dramatic change all over Europe' instead, it would be classed as a relative clause because it would contain a verb. However, either version is grammatically acceptable. An example such as this simply shows how subtle these distinctions can be.

Adverbial clauses and participle clauses

Some subordinate clauses, known as adverbial clauses, *modify* the verb phrase in the main clause. That is to say, they explain how, when, where or why the subject in the main clause did whatever they did. Here are some examples:

Example 1

Florence took her shoes off <u>as soon as she arrived home</u>.

In this example, the action denoted by the verb *took* in the main clause is the removal of Florence's shoes. The adverbial clause following the main clause modifies this verb by explaining to the reader *when* it took place, namely when Florence arrived home.

Example 2

<u>Determined that her next shot would hit its target</u>, the archer aimed carefully.

In this example, the action denoted by the verb *aimed* in the main clause is the careful focus of the archer on her target. We know that the focus is careful in nature because the verb is accompanied by the adverb, or modifier, *carefully*. The adverbial clause before the main clause further modifies this verb phrase by explaining *why* the archer aimed carefully.

Example 3

Derek unpacked the components and, <u>ensuring that he followed the instructions to the letter</u>, he successfully assembled his new wardrobe.

In this example, an adverbial clause has been embedded between two main clauses. It is modifying the verb in the second of the two main clauses by explaining *how* the wardrobe was *assembled*. This is a specific type of adverbial clause called a <u>participle clause</u> because it begins with the <u>participle</u> form of the verb *ensure*. In this case, it is a <u>present participle</u>, which, like most present participles, ends in the *-ing* suffix.

Example 4

However, some participle clauses begin with the past participle form of a verb (many, but not all of which end with *ed* or *en*), e.g.:

<u>**Confused by the signpost**</u>**, Connor went the wrong way.**

This is still an adverbial clause since it modifies the verb *went* (it tells us *why* Connor went the wrong way).

Example 5

Here is another example of a sentence that contains a participle clause:

Faris shook hands with his opponent, <u>disappointed though he was with the result</u>.

Example 6

Often, the subject of a subordinate clause is contained within, but sometimes it is <u>implied</u>. That is to say, the thing or person acting as the subject in the clause is obvious from the context, e.g.:

Mrs Smith thanked her friend for the biscuit, <u>politely declining a second</u>.

In the example above, the subject is not included in the subordinate clause itself because it isn't necessary. It is obvious that the person declining a second biscuit is Mrs Smith. This is called an <u>implied subject</u>, about which you can read more in Appendix 6, page 191.

Example 7

Here is another example of an implied subject:

The birthday card, <u>sent to him by his aunt</u>, contained a £5 note.

In the example above, the subject and object in the participle clause have been reversed so that it is written in the passive voice. You can find out more about active and passive clauses in Chapter 16, 'Moods and voices', page 153.

Comment clauses

Comment clauses are probably the most common type of subordinate clause that people use when they're talking aloud. They are added to a main clause as a means of packaging the information for the reader or listener. They are often somewhat inconsequential but they assist a speaker or a writer in making their audience more receptive to their words. Here are some common examples:

<u>**To be honest**</u>**, I don't think he even wanted the job.**
The 5:23 train will be our best bet, <u>I'd have thought</u>.
<u>**You must admit**</u>**, that was an impressive performance.**

<u>I have a feeling that</u> it's going to rain later.

He hasn't been very well lately <u>as I'm sure you're aware</u>.

Very often, clauses like this provide qualification to what is being said and they're especially common alongside utterances that might cause controversy or disagreement, as a way of softening their impact.

Subordinate interrogative clauses

An interrogative clause is a posh way of saying 'a question'. A straightforward question such as *'What is your name?'* would be a main interrogative clause or, assuming that it stands on its own, an interrogative sentence. However, we sometimes add a subordinate clause to a main clause that *turns it into* a question. Here are some examples:

<u>Would you mind if</u> I take this chair?

You don't have any children, <u>do you</u>?

<u>Is it true that</u> you met the Queen?

We're friends, <u>aren't we</u>?

Notice that in the absence of the interrogative clause, the main clauses in all of these sentences would merely be statements. The second and fourth follow a structure that we all use every day, in which we make a statement and then effectively invite the reader or listener to deny it by asking about its reverse. It's a very strange way to communicate when you stop to think about it, but then that's the case with much of English grammar, **isn't it?**

Teaching ideas

As complex and compound sentences are first introduced in Key Stage 2 in the National Curriculum, all of the suggestions are aimed at Key Stage 2 pupils. For more ideas about how to introduce subordinating and coordinating conjunctions to Key Stage 1 pupils, head to Chapter 9, 'Main and subordinate clauses'.

Hot seat interrogation

You're probably familiar with hot seating as a tool for exploring characters in texts. For those who haven't used it before, a child sits at the front of the class and takes on the role of a character from a novel or a historical figure. The rest of the class then ask the child questions, which they answer in character. You'll find that children often ask questions like 'How old are you?' or 'Do you have any family?' In this version, brainstorm your questions beforehand and challenge your class to use subordinate interrogative clauses when they write their questions, e.g. *'Is it true that you buried your Parmesan cheese during the Great Fire of London, Mr Pepys?'*

LKS2 **UKS2**

Match the clauses

Use this as a chance to revise key historical figures with your class while teaching them about how to embed a clause. Provide them with a set of simple sentences and a set of subordinate clauses about different people from history (you can use the following set, which is also provided on a worksheet in the online resources). Your pupils have to match the sentence to the relative clause, drawing on their historical knowledge, e.g.:

William Shakespeare, whose plays have been performed all over the world, was born in Stratford-upon-Avon.

Once pupils have decided which clauses go together, ask them to write out the sentences, paying close attention to how they punctuate to link the clauses.

Clauses to match

Main clause	Subordinate clause
Henry VIII married six times.	Who created beautiful oil paintings
Florence Nightingale was a nurse in the Crimean War.	By refusing to give up her seat on the bus
Mary Jackson became the first African-American female engineer at NASA.	Whose work included developing the theory of radioactivity
Charles Dickens based his characters on people in his life.	Who wrote *A Christmas Carol*
Marie Curie was the first woman to win a Nobel Prize.	Having overcome extreme prejudice because of the colour of her skin
Van Gogh cut off his own ear.	Known as 'The Lady with the Lamp'
Rosa Parks became known as 'The First Lady of Civil Rights'.	Whose first divorce caused the Protestant Reformation

 LKS2 **UKS2**

Sort the sentences

Look at the sentences below and read them as a class. There is a downloadable version of the sentences in the online resources, which you can either print or display on a whiteboard. Explain that some of them are simple sentences, some are compound and others are complex. Ask your pupils to try to sort out the sentences into the three categories.

1. Alice's parents sold their house.
2. Despite being all-powerful, Voldemort still couldn't conjure up a nose.
3. We need to go to the shops because we are out of milk.

4. I would love to come to the cinema but I am busy this afternoon.

5. The frog ate flies and other insects.

6. When I was little, I wanted to be a train driver.

7. The man screamed; his finger was trapped in the car door.

8. The Queen took her corgi to the vet after realising it was ill.

9. Mrs Trunchbull was big and Matilda was small.

10. Tottenham Hotspur are the best football team in the country.

These sentences are too simple

UKS2

Read the extract below as a class and explain that it is written entirely in simple sentences. There is a downloadable version of the text in the online resources, which you can either print or display on a whiteboard. Discuss the effect that repeated simple sentences have on the reader: the writing becomes repetitive and monotonous. Challenge your pupils to rewrite the extract using complex, compound and simple sentences. Once they have finished, choose a few pupils to read their improved extract out to the class, and discuss the sentence structure choices they have made. You could simplify this activity for younger pupils by breaking up the text into a series of separate sentences and asking them to add a subordinate clause to each one.

Extract

It was a beautiful day. Clare and Olivia went to the beach. They wanted to go swimming. They chose the best place on the sand. They unfolded their towels. Then they started to put on sun cream. Clare walked down to the water's edge. She dipped her toe in apprehensively. Suddenly she screamed. There was something approaching her in the water. It was big and grey. It had a large, pointed fin. Clare ran out of the sea as fast as she could.

Spot the subordinate clauses

UKS2

As we said at the beginning of the chapter, the only type of subordinate clause that the Department for Education expects children to be able to name in the Year 6 grammar, punctuation and spelling test is a relative clause. However, if you think that your class are ready to take on a bit more, you could explore the modelled text on the following page (also available as a worksheet in the online resources). Agree on a key and ask them to highlight the different types of clauses. You could extend this activity further by getting your class to continue the text.

Modelled text

Having finished her dinner, Jessica went upstairs to her room. It had been a long day and she was quite relieved when her mum suggested she get an early night. Suddenly, there was a knock at her bedroom door.

'Do you mind if I come in?' a muffled voice called through the door.

Jessica, unsure whom to expect, tentatively opened the door. Standing in front of her was her friend Nyla.

'Nyla! What are you doing here?'

'I wanted to check you were OK, after what happened.'

'I'm OK or, at least, I will be. It's only a stupid part in a play after all.'

'For what it's worth, I think you should have got the part.'

'Thanks, Nyla.'

Before they had a chance to say anything else, Jessica's younger brother burst out of his room.

Chapter 11

Prepositions and conjunctions

Chapter overview

In this chapter we'll make the case for ditching the connectives. (2010 called; they want their lazy grammar definitions back.) We'll also look at:

• The role of prepositions in a sentence.	LKS2	Pages 112–113
• The difference between subordinating and coordinating conjunctions.	UKS2	Pages 113–115
• Ideas and resources to support teaching of these concepts.	KS1	Pages 115–117
	LKS2	
	UKS2	

At this point, we need to bring in our final two word classes. In Part 1, we looked at nouns, pronouns, determiners, verbs, adjectives and adverbs. In this chapter, we are going to explore the role of prepositions and conjunctions in forming sentences. Prepositions and conjunctions are joining words. They tend to link the other items in a sentence together and clarify the connections or relationships between them. Before we dive in, it's worth saying a few words about one bad grammatical idea that has been very hard to kill: the tyranny of the *connective*.

Cut the connectives

Before the current obsession in this country's education system with fronted adverbials, determiners and exclamation sentences, we teachers sometimes like to imagine that we inhabited a perpetually sunlit paradise totally free from arbitrary grammar rules. And then we remember connectives. You won't find them in the glossary of grammar terms that children learn in the National Curriculum anymore and, while there may be much to criticise in the current regime, this is something to be celebrated.

'Connectives' was a term whose main function was to confuse primary school teachers and their pupils about writing. It was a term that was used to cover <u>conjunctions</u> such as *and*, *or* and *but*. It was also used to describe <u>fronted time adverbs</u> such as *first*, *next*, *secondly* and *finally*. Some teachers would tell their pupils that relative pronouns such as *when* and *which* were connectives. It was also used to describe <u>discourse markers</u> such as *furthermore*, *alternatively* and even entire phrases such as *on the other hand* that were dumped in the overflowing bin labelled 'connectives'. These words serve very different grammatical functions, and just teaching them to children as though they are one concept does not simplify things, as is sometimes suggested. It causes utter confusion. It can't be stressed often enough when it comes to grammar: **you can't simplify something by teaching it incorrectly**. Ditch the connectives. They won't help you to teach grammar and they won't help your pupils learn to write.

What you need to know

So, if we aren't teaching children about connectives, what should we be teaching them instead? Well, many of the roles ascribed to connectives by teachers in the last 20 years are fulfilled by two very useful classes of word: prepositions and conjunctions. Let's explore them one at a time.

Prepositions

What are prepositions? Well, the clue is in the name. The simplest place to start is to break the word in two: **pre – position.** The prefix *pre-* is often used to mean *before*. In many sentences, a preposition is the word that is found before a position. Here are a couple of examples:

The cat is <u>on</u> the mat.

The mat is the cat's current position – that's where the cat is. What word comes before *the mat* in this sentence? *On.* So, *on* is the preposition.

My shoes were <u>under</u> the table.

The table is the shoes' current position – that's where the shoes are. The preposition *under* clarifies this somewhat to explain exactly where in relation to the table they are. Words like *on*, *in*, *by*, *above*, *below*, *around*, *inside*, *over*, *under*, *beyond*, *behind*, *between*, *towards*, *beneath*, *within*, etc. are prepositions when used in this way. However, prepositions don't only deal with physical positions or places; they also deal with time. Consider this example:

Drinks were served <u>during</u> the reception <u>after</u> the wedding ceremony.

This sentence contains two prepositions that deal with time. They indicate not *where* one object is relative to another, but rather *when* one event took place relative to another. Many of the same prepositions that we use to talk about place can also be used to talk about time (*on* Tuesday, *in* 1997, *at* night, *between* Christmas and Easter, etc.), but some (like *during* and *after*) are fairly unique to matters of chronology.

As well as indicating relationships of space and time, prepositions can indicate more abstract relationships between the elements in a sentence. Consider these examples:

This is a gift <u>for</u> my friend.

Hamlet was written <u>by</u> William Shakespeare.

The frog turned <u>into</u> a princess.

The cash machine is <u>out of</u> money.

Notice that, in the final sentence, a pair of prepositions is used to express the relationship. It is quite common for prepositions to appear in twos or sometimes even threes:

The car is parked <u>next to</u> the tree.

February is <u>in between</u> January and March.

That subordinate clause could go <u>in front of</u> the main clause.

Conjunctions

Conjunctions create logical connections between the elements in a sentence. The simplest and most obvious examples are probably *and*, *but*, *or*, *if* and *because*, all of which are usually used as conjunctions. However, conjunctions are deceptive little things. They seem incredibly simple at first glance but there is in fact an awful lot of complexity here. For a start, there are two types of conjunction: <u>coordinating conjunctions</u> and <u>subordinating conjunctions</u>. Let's explore these one at a time and unpick some of the tricky issues that come with them.

Coordinating conjunctions

Coordinating conjunctions are used to create a logical link between two equally important parts of a sentence. These could be individual words, phrases or clauses. There are generally considered to be seven coordinating conjunctions in the English language: *for*, *and*, *nor*, *but*, *or*, *yet* and *so* (lots of teachers use the mnemonic FANBOYS to help their pupils remember them). In the following examples, the coordinating conjunction creates a logical link between two individual words or names:

Peter <u>and</u> Paul were going to school.

You must hand this letter to your mother <u>or</u> your father.

I am neither a butcher <u>nor</u> a baker.

In each of the sentences above, the coordinating conjunction separates individual words that, together, form either the subject or the object of a simple sentence. Note that, in each case, the two words are of equal importance to the meaning of the sentence. In some sentences, a coordinating conjunction is used to join two phrases together:

Swift as an eagle <u>and</u> *light as a feather*, **the dragonfly darted over the pond.**
The hotel is *great for young couples* <u>but</u> *far from ideal for families with children.*
The weather that morning was *wonderfully bright* <u>yet</u> *strangely chilly.*

In the sentences above, the phrases linked by the underlined conjunctions have been italicised. Once again, you'll notice that they are equally important to the meaning of the sentence. There isn't one that obviously matters more in terms of understanding the author's meaning. Coordinating conjunctions are also used to link two main clauses. This happens in instances where it would be perfectly acceptable to place a full stop and a capital letter but in which the writer prefers to establish a logical connection between the main clauses by using a conjunction:

I do not have an umbrella <u>so</u> **I do not want to go out in the rain.**
I will go to the party <u>but</u> **I will not stay for long.**
You must not climb over this fence <u>for</u> **only a fool plays on the railway line.**

Once again, what makes these coordinating conjunctions is the fact that the two main clauses separated by them are of equal importance to understanding the meaning of the sentence.

Subordinating conjunctions

While coordinating conjunctions are used to link two equally weighted elements of a sentence, subordinating conjunctions are used to link two elements where one is less important than the other – typically by linking a main clause to a subordinate clause or a phrase. There are many more words that can be used as subordinating conjunctions than coordinating conjunctions and, to complicate matters further, many prepositions and coordinating conjunctions can also be used as subordinating conjunctions! Some of the most common subordinating conjunctions are *after, although, as, because, before, despite, if, since, until, when, whereas* and *while*. Some subordinating conjunctions consist of more than one word, such as *in order to* or *given that*. Let's take a look at some examples.

Example 1

Harry is moving to Ireland <u>because</u> **his mum has got a new job there.**

In this sentence, both clauses matter but one matters more than the other. The primary purpose of this sentence is to inform the reader that Harry's mum is moving to Ireland, not that his mum has got a new job. For this reason, *because* is a subordinating conjunction, indicating the start of a subordinate clause.

Example 2

<u>**Even though**</u> **she tried her best, Molly didn't win the competition.**

In this example, two words are behaving as a subordinating conjunction and they are found at the front of the sentence. The main piece of information the author wishes to convey is that Molly didn't win the competition. The further information – which assures us that she tried her best – is subordinate to the main clause. The words *even though* establish a logical relationship between the two pieces of information.

Example 3

I'll go <u>if</u> you do.

This example is perhaps less clear cut than the others. Children are often inclined to think of 'if' as a coordinating conjunction because the clauses on either side can look equally important. However, if you think about the purpose of this sentence, I am stating the conditions upon which I'll go to wherever it is you want me to go. Therefore 'I'll go' is the main clause and 'if you do' is subordinate to it. This is a bit more obvious if you change the circumstances slightly:

Arthur was willing to go <u>if</u> his wife was.

Understanding the difference between coordinating and subordinating conjunctions is useful for children in developing the range of sentence structures they are able to employ, as well as helping them to use punctuation appropriately – especially commas. You can read more about how to use commas to link clauses in Chapter 13, page 127.

Teaching ideas

At present, prepositions are part of the Key Stage 2 curriculum, so the teaching ideas on prepositions are aimed at Year 3 upwards. By the end of Key Stage 1, children are expected to be using the subordinating conjunctions *when*, *if*, *that* and *because*, as well as the coordinating conjunctions *and*, *or* and *but*. Most of the activities on conjunctions can be adapted to fit the Key Stage 1 and Key Stage 2 curriculum requirements.

Add the conjunctions

Provide your class with a range of different sentences and ask them to complete the sentence with an appropriate conjunction. Once they have finished, choose a few pupils to read their sentences to the class and discuss the conjunctions they chose. Did anyone use a different conjunction? How does that change the meaning of the sentence? In some cases, there will be right and wrong answers but, in others, there is a discussion to be had about how word choices affect meaning. There are separate resources for Key Stage 1 and Key Stage 2 to use for this activity on the next page, which are also provided as printable worksheets in the online resources.

Key Stage 1 resource

The children were not allowed out to play _____ it was raining.
_____ the weather is nice, we will go to the beach tomorrow.
You can have jelly babies _____ a chocolate bar.
The postman delivers letters _____ packages.
She was so excited _____ she couldn't sleep.
Mum said he could play outside _____ he had finished his dinner.
I wanted to go to the cinema _____ the tickets had sold out.
The cat likes to eat tuna _____ salmon.

Key Stage 2 resource

You can't watch TV _____ eating your dinner.
You can have pudding _____ a starter _____ not both.
Jacob has not done his homework _____ he has tidied his room.
Fatimah has got ten stickers _____ Martha only has four.
_____ the film had finished, they went to a restaurant for dinner.
_____ she was far away, she could hear every word they were saying.
_____ the tiger approached its prey, it growled softly.
We cannot buy that _____ it is too expensive.
Remember to brush your teeth _____ you go to bed.
'It's a long time _____ I've seen him,' he said.
I would like to buy three chocolate bars _____ a bag of liquorice _____
I do not have enough money.
He appeared calm _____ the imminent danger.
_____ you finish your peas, you can have pudding.
We are not going out to play _____ somebody owns up.
My teacher is strict _____ kind.

LKS2 ## Where is it?

Get yourself a puppet or a cuddly toy and place it on a desk. Ask your class, 'Where is the cuddly toy?' and listen to their responses. Write 'The cuddly toy is on the table.' on the board and underline the word 'on'. Choose different children to move the cuddly toy to different places, while the rest of the class write down the sentence explaining where the cuddly toy is using the appropriate preposition.

Record a preposition rap

LKS2
UKS2

There are a number of examples of preposition songs on YouTube (this is a good one: www. youtube.com/watch?v=byszemY8Pl8). A preposition rap is incredibly simple to make. All you need is a repetitive beat and a long list of prepositions. Record your class chanting the prepositions over the beat and hey presto – you have a preposition rap. Chanting is an effective way of committing words to memory, so the process of practising and performing the rap will help those prepositions stick!

Preposition countdown

LKS2
UKS2

Split the class into pairs. Write the preposition(s) to be used on the board. You might just want to start with one to begin with, e.g. 'below'. Explain that the aim is to write as many complete sentences using the preposition as possible before the time runs out. You'll know how much time is challenging for your class but if you're feeling particularly mean you could use the *Countdown* clock.

Change the conjunctions

LKS2
UKS2

Use the modelled text below and find the subordinating and coordinating conjunctions as a class. Once you have found all of them, challenge your class to rewrite the text with different conjunctions. Discuss how this could change the meaning of the extract and how only some conjunctions would be appropriate. There is a worksheet available for this activity in the online resources, which includes a copy of the modelled text.

Modelled text

The cat curled up in front of the glow of the fire and began to purr loudly. It had been a long day. She had hoped there would be some tuna for dinner but it had been sardines. The heat from the fire was intense yet comforting at the same time. The cat didn't mind. She would stay here until somebody moved her. A little while later, her human wandered into the lounge carrying a book and a cup of tea. He bent down by the fire and poked it until the flames were large and moving wildly. Until then, the cat had been quite content. Now she backed away from the fire and retreated to the sofa. She knew the fire could be dangerous because of what had happened at Christmas.

Describe the scene

LKS2
UKS2

Put the children in pairs. Explain that one of them is going to have their eyes closed while the other one watches a short video clip and describes what is happening. Ask your pupils to focus on using prepositions, e.g. 'A man is walking along the corridor.' If you are not sure where to get such a clip from, the Literacy Shed has some fantastic videos you can use.

Chapter 12

Types of phrase

Chapter overview

Phrases are the building blocks that make up sentences. Sort of like word Lego™. And who doesn't love Lego? In this chapter we will look at:

• How to use and identify noun phrases.	KS1	Page 120
• How to use and identify verb phrases.	LKS2	Page 121
• How to use and identify adjective and adverbial phrases.	UKS2	Pages 122–123
• How to use and identify prepositional phrases.	UKS2	Page 123
• Ideas and resources to support teaching of these concepts.	KS1 LKS2 UKS2	Pages 123–126

We use the word 'phrase' informally to refer to any short example of language. 'What a lovely turn of phrase,' we might say, or 'Let me rephrase this.' Indeed, a phrase is a very useful unit of language for teaching children about editing and improving their writing. In a sentence like 'The cat sat on the mat', I have the beginnings of three phrases, which I can expand infinitely: 'My grandma's ginger cat had sat down contentedly on the large, grey mat.' By seeing the phrases in their sentences, and editing them one at a time, your pupils will be able to improve and enhance their own writing – saving you an awful lot of work!

What you need to know

A phrase is a group of words that has an individual function in a sentence. For example:

A group of explorers decided to climb an exceptionally large mountain.

This sentence is composed of three phrases: a verb phrase sandwiched between two noun phrases. The noun phrase *A group of explorers* serves as the subject of this sentence. It is composed of four words but it serves a single function in the sentence: it tells us who is going to be climbing a mountain. The verb phrase *decided to climb* tells us what the group of explorers is doing to the mountain. Once again, it is a group of words serving a single function. Finally, the noun phrase *an exceptionally large mountain*, the object of the sentence, tells us what the group of explorers decided to climb. Now compare the sentence to the following example:

They climbed Everest.

Notice that this sentence has the same structure and a similar meaning but each of the three functions in the sentence is now served by a single word. Very often, a phrase is an expanded and modified version of a single word in which that word itself is either included or replaced. This idea might start to make a little more sense if we begin with perhaps the simplest type of phrase: the noun phrase.

Noun phrases

A noun phrase is a group of words that serves the same function as a noun in a sentence (see Chapter 2, page 23, for more on nouns). Often, but not always, a noun phrase will serve as either the subject or the object of a clause. Here are some examples:

I love funny, light-hearted films.

In this noun phrase, two adjectives (*funny* and *light-hearted*) have been used to modify the noun *films* to give it a more specific meaning.

It felt like any other day.

In this noun phrase, two determiners (*any* and *other*) have been used to modify the meaning of the noun *day*.

We serve the best cake in Britain.

In this noun phrase, the definite article *the*, the superlative adjective *best*, the preposition *in* and the proper noun *Britain* have been used to advertise and promote the *cake* that is being served. The entire phrase forms the object of the sentence.

Verb phrases

Rather than containing a single verb, many clauses contain an entire verb phrase that conveys a more nuanced meaning or specifies a particular tense:

I <u>wish I could have been</u> a fly on the wall in that meeting.

In this sentence, a complex series of modal and auxiliary verbs expresses the relatively complicated relationship between the writer and the notion of being a fly on the wall in the meeting. It tells us a number of things: that the meeting has already taken place, that the writer wasn't present in the meeting and that they would like to have heard what was said in the meeting. Selecting the right verb phrase is very important for ensuring succinct writing. See Chapter 4, 'Types of verb', page 45, for more on modal verbs and auxiliary verbs.

In English, we often end up creating incredibly complicated verb phrases without really thinking about it and we convey all sort of nuance as a result. Consider the various effects created by these verb phrases:

I <u>don't believe I've ever spoken</u> to Victoria.

He <u>wouldn't have expected to receive</u> that sort of welcome.

She <u>had been watching and waiting</u> for quite some time.

In all of these examples, the verb phrase acts as the main verb in the clause – describing how the subject behaves. However, this is not true of all verb phrases. <u>De-tensed verb phrases</u> are phrases without a subject and without a specific tense, which are understood in relation to the items in the main clause:

The referee approached the player, <u>brandishing a red card</u>.

<u>Huffing and puffing</u>, the wolf blew the house down.

The company's new games console, <u>released last month</u>, has enjoyed great success.

There is a blurred line between verb phrases like these and subordinate clauses. In a sense, however, establishing exactly where that line falls isn't too important, since the punctuation conventions associated with them are the same either way. If the verb phrase follows on from the main clause, no punctuation is usually required. A fronted verb phrase would usually be separated from the main clause with a comma. An embedded verb phrase would usually have commas at either end.

The other common type of verb phrase worth mentioning is known as a <u>gerund</u>. This is a verb phrase (usually involving a present participle ending in -*ing*) that functions as a noun and that can form the subject or object of a sentence. Consider this sentence:

<u>Staying at home</u> beats <u>going to work</u>.

Staying at home is the subject of this sentence and *going to work* is the object. Both of these are gerunds; they are verb phrases but they are 'behaving' like nouns.

Adjective phrases

An adjective phrase, or adjectival phrase, is a group of words that replaces and expands an adjective, modifying its meaning. In other words, it is a phrase that offers a description of a noun. Here is a simple example:

The film was <u>disappointingly predictable</u>.

The adjective phrase at the end of this sentence describes *the film*. In this case, an adverb has been placed before an adjective to make it into an adjective phrase. This is extremely common and we use phrases like this all the time – *terribly sorry, totally wrong, surprisingly good*, etc.

A lot of similes take the form of adjective phrases – standing in place of a single adjective:

He was <u>as cunning as a fox</u>.

This writer could have simply chosen to say 'he was cunning' but has instead chosen to expand the adjective into a phrase. The same has happened in this example:

Amsterdam, <u>famous for its canals and consistently popular with tourists</u>, is one of the most beautiful cities in Europe.

In this instance, the two adjectives *famous* and *popular* have been combined and expanded to offer more specific information about what Amsterdam is famous for and whom it's popular with.

Adverbial phrases

An adverbial phrase, quite simply, is a phrase that serves the same function as an adverb in a clause. That is to say, it describes where, when, how or why the main verb in the clause was enacted.

She leapt from her seat <u>without a moment's hesitation</u>.

An adverb like *quickly* or *suddenly* would serve the same function as this phrase, which is to modify the verb *leapt*. In this instance, the phrase indicates the speed with which she leapt. Any word or phrase that modifies the meaning of a verb can be described as adverbial.

<u>After dinner</u>, I played a game with my brother.

In this example, we have the famous fronted adverbial: a phrase that modifies the verb *played* by explaining *when* the playing took place. Many of the adverbial phrases we use are very simple structures of this sort that establish where and when something happened: *on Saturday, at school, last year, on the way home*, etc. Many of these are also classed as prepositional phrases (see page 123).

Above, we observed that many similes take the form of adjective phrases. Many other similes take the form of adverbial phrases:

She dashed down the home straight <u>as fast as a startled gazelle</u>.

This phrase is modifying the verb *dashed*, which makes it adverbial. However, you may have noticed that there is a noun phrase (*a startled gazelle*) contained within the adverbial phrase. There are some really grey areas when it comes to classifying types of phrase and you will often find phrases that can fit into more than one category.

Prepositional phrases

To cut a long story short, prepositional phrases are phrases that begin with a preposition. They act as <u>complements</u> (for more on complements, see Appendix 5, page 189) and they modify the meaning of a clause. Here are some examples:

I'm going to build the shed <u>with Alex</u>.

I drew a picture <u>of a cat</u>.

<u>For my birthday</u>, I would like a puppy.

I'm absolutely furious <u>with them</u>.

<u>On the whole</u>, it was a fairly good book.

Once again, you will notice a blurring of the boundaries between these phrases and some of the other categories of phrase. In particular, some of these look decidedly adverbial!

Teaching ideas

According to the National Curriculum, phrases should be introduced in Year 2, starting with noun phrases. The other phrases covered in this chapter are all part of the current Key Stage 2 curriculum.

Write a noun phrase

KS1

Photocopy and cut out two copies of the cards in the online resources and put them face down on a table. You can preview the cards on the next page. Each child is to take a card, stick it in their book and come up with as many different noun phrases as they can for that noun. For example:

> ## Castle

The oldest castle in Britain
The cold and draughty castle
The looming castle
His favourite castle
The Queen's castle

Cards

Pigeon	Castle	Cat	Pirate	Apple
Bear	Girl	Teacher	Baby	Parrot
Cheese	Tree	Garden	Photograph	Play

 KS1

Describe the picture

Show your class a variety of images and ask them to describe them to a partner. Then get them to choose one image to stick in their book to generate noun phrases about. The website www.onceuponapicture.co.uk has an excellent collection of images for this activity in their 'Character Collection'.

LKS2

How/when/where did they do it?

UKS2

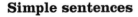

This is an activity for teaching adverbial phrases. Give out the following list of simple sentences and ask your class to add a relevant adverbial phrase to each one. They can decide whether to put the phrase at the beginning or at the end of the sentence. Choose a few children to share their finished work and discuss the decisions they made. There is a printable worksheet for this activity available online.

Simple sentences

The dog dribbled.
The rocket landed.
I drove my car.
She opened the door.
He jumped over the hurdle.
The llama licked its lips.
They played a board game.
We went out for dinner.

LKS2

Act it out!

UKS2

Sit in a circle and choose a child to act out a hobby they enjoy. It could be anything: playing tennis, swimming, athletics. Ask the rest of the class to describe HOW they are doing the action, using an adverbial or prepositional phrase, e.g. *'He is swimming in a cold pool.'*

Find the phrases

LKS2
UKS2

Use the modelled text below and agree on a class key for the different types of phrase. Read it through and give your pupils time to highlight the different types of phrase. Once pupils have identified them, challenge them to replace the original phrases with their own phrases. How does this change the meaning of the text? There is a printable worksheet with this text available in the online resources.

Modelled text

Cautiously and carefully, Elizabeth shuffled across the marble floor. She knew she wasn't supposed to be in the museum alone; her grandmother would be furious if she were to find out. Clutching the precious item and her grandmother's walking stick, she tiptoed up the stairs. She had assumed nobody would miss this dull, tarnished pot. Most of the visitors to the museum hardly gave it a second glance. Surely, it would be better with somebody who would actually appreciate it? She continued up the cold, hard staircase, being careful not to make a sound. Once she reached the top, she breathed a sigh of relief. The office was just three metres away. Above the door hung the brass key to the office door. Her grandma put it up there so it was out of her reach. All she had to do was creep down the corridor, knock the key off the hook using the walking stick and her mission would be complete. She put her foot on the thick, green carpet, stepping as lightly as possible.
    'Elizabeth Alexandra Morris! What on EARTH do you think you are doing?'

Prepositional phrase walk

LKS2
UKS2

Take a walk around the school grounds and document it with photographs. Back in the classroom, ask the class to recap the walk using prepositional phrases, e.g. *'We walked through the classroom door. Then we walked down the corridor.'* Alternatively you could use the book *Rosie's Walk* by Pat Hutchins (2009) and describe Rosie's walk through the farm. Although this text is aimed at slightly younger children, it is full of prepositional phrases!

Write your own

LKS2
UKS2

Use this process with your class to get them writing their own sentences, including prepositional phrases:

1. Write a simple sentence:

The swimming pool was cold.

2. Add a prepositional phrase:

The swimming pool was cold in the morning.

3. Add another prepositional phrase to the beginning of the sentence and add a comma:

In the summer, the swimming pool was cold in the morning.

 There is a template provided below (and there is a printable version in the online resources) to support children with this activity.

Template

   1. Write a simple sentence:

      _____

   2. Add one prepositional phrase:

      _____

   3. Add another prepositional phrase to the beginning of the sentence and add a comma:

      _____

UKS2 Identify the verb phrases

There are a number of online quizzes on verb phrases (yes, really). This is a particularly good one for children in Years 5 and 6: www.proprofs.com/quiz-school/story.php?title=verb-verb-phrases. Put it up on the interactive whiteboard and get different pairs of children to come and identify the verb phrase in the sentence. Make sure you ask them how they know the answer as well as what the answer is.

Chapter 13

Commas

Chapter overview

One of the title ideas for this book was 'Where Do the Commas Go?', as this is an area of grammar many adults find difficult. (If you have any adults in your life who struggle with commas, do them and us a favour and buy them a copy of this book.) In this chapter we will look at:

• How to use commas to separate items in a list.	KS1	Pages 128–129
• How to use commas to embed, parenthesise and offset negations, to attribute quotations and direct speech, and to indicate who is being addressed.	LKS2	Pages 129–132
• Ideas and resources to support teaching of these concepts.	KS1 LKS2 UKS2	Pages 132–134

You are probably familiar with the famous joke that gave Lynne Truss's (2009) equally famous grammar book *Eats, Shoots and Leaves* its title. If not, it goes something like this: a panda walks into a bar and orders a burger. After he finishes the burger, the panda draws a pistol and fires several shots, causing the other customers in the bar to cower in terror, before departing. One of the customers asks the bartender why the panda behaved in such a way, to which the bartender replies:

He's a panda. He eats, shoots and leaves.

The basis of this joke, of course, is the comma between the word *eats* and the word *shoots*. Without the comma, we would understand the second sentence in the punchline as consisting of a subject (*he*), a single verb (*eats*) and an object comprised of two nouns separated by a coordinating conjunction (*shoots and leaves*). However, with the comma, the grammar of the sentence changes completely. We now interpret *eats*, *shoots* and *leaves* as three separate verbs, the comma indicating that they are items in a list.

Commas matter and they can seriously confuse the reader when used incorrectly. Most literate adults of working age now, whose formal grammar education was pretty minimal, have absorbed their understanding of how to use commas organically, but there are still many lingering misconceptions and many common mistakes that both teachers and pupils are prone to making. As a consequence, too many educators still resort to talking about commas as 'pauses' or places to 'take a short breath'. They will say things like 'a comma is a shorter pause than a full stop'. This is all utter twaddle: many commas are used in places where no pause at all is required, while others are used in places where a far longer pause is needed than the average breath between two sentences. Commas indicate specific features of a sentence's grammar – they have nothing whatsoever to do with breathing!

What you need to know

So, having established what the role of commas is not, let's consider what it is. A comma <u>offsets</u> (separates) one part of a sentence from another and there are several reasons why we might want to do this.

Separating items in a list

This is the only 'rule' that many adults were explicitly taught about using commas when they were at school and, for many teachers, it is often the only one they're confident teaching. When listing a <u>series of items</u>, we typically place a comma in between each item apart from the last two, between which we place a coordinating conjunction – usually *and* or *or*.

The United Kingdom comprises <u>England, Scotland, Wales and Northern Ireland</u>.
I packed <u>three pairs of socks, four pairs of underpants, one pair of trousers and two shirts</u>.
<u>Please could you hand this to Tom, Dick or Harry?</u>

This convention is fairly straightforward and most children find it reasonably easy to understand. The only complication is caused by the <u>Oxford comma</u>: an entirely optional comma in between the penultimate item in the list and the coordinating conjunction. For example:

I went to the park with my two dogs, Nick, and Simon.

Proponents of the Oxford comma argue that it eliminates <u>ambiguity</u> in situations where a sentence can have two very different meanings. In the above sentence, it seems clear that the writer went to the park with two dogs and two people called Nick and Simon. However, if you remove the Oxford comma, this becomes less clear:

I went to the park with my two dogs, Nick and Simon.

In this version of the sentence, it now appears that the comma may be for <u>parenthesis</u> (see page 129) and that the two dogs are called Nick and Simon. However, opponents of the Oxford comma point out that there are just as many situations where it can actually introduce ambiguity. For example, look what happens if we have only one dog:

I went to the park with my dog, Nick, and Simon.

It's now impossible to say whether Nick is the name of the dog or a separate person. There have been some surprisingly heated debates about the Oxford comma over the years but the good news is that both approaches are entirely acceptable. It's usually possible to eliminate ambiguity altogether by giving careful thought to the order in which you list items in a sentence:

I went to the park with Nick, Simon and my two dogs.

or

I went to the park with Simon and my dog, Nick.

Separating fronted adverbials and subordinate clauses from the main clause

Subordinate clauses, phrases and individual words placed before the main clause are usually separated off with a comma. Here are some examples:

Regrettably, I shall have to decline your offer.	Fronted adverb
Without a doubt, this is the finest restaurant in town.	Fronted prepositional phrase
When he'd finished his homework, Oliver went to bed.	Fronted adverbial clause

These commas can be very important in terms of eliminating ambiguity. Consider this sentence:

Most of the time, travellers in London enjoy their stay.

If you remove the comma between the adverbial phrase and the main clause in this sentence, you alter it dramatically, turning it into a sentence about time travellers in London!

It's usually perfectly acceptable to separate a subordinate clause that follows on from a main clause with a comma too – but it isn't quite as common:

Sophie returned home in order to feed the cat.
Sophie returned home, in order to feed the cat.

Both of these are perfectly acceptable forms but the comma is not as essential as it would be if the subordinate clause had come first.

Embedding, parenthesis and offsetting negations

When we embed a word, a phrase or a subordinate clause within a main clause, we place commas either side of it. Here are some examples:

Amy, <u>who loved cats</u>, drew a picture of a kitten.	Embedded relative clause
Paul, <u>hungry and exhausted</u>, finally gave in.	Embedded adjective phrase
The shop, <u>sadly</u>, has had to close.	Embedded adverb

Embedded words, phrases and clauses are often a form of <u>parenthesis</u>, clarifying or elaborating on a person or an object that has just been mentioned, e.g.:

My brother, <u>William,</u> lives in Scotland.

In this case, a comma for parenthesis has been placed after the subject *my brother* to introduce the extra information (the brother's name), and another comma has been included after *William* to indicate that the interruption to the main clause has finished. However, a comma for parenthesis can also be found at the end of a main clause, often indicating that further information is about to be given about the object of the sentence:

I completed this project with Connor, <u>a boy in my class.</u>

We use commas in a similar way to introduce negations, usually phrases that begin with the word *not*:

It is the Queen, <u>not the King</u>, who really wields power in this land.
I decided to go to Spain, <u>not France</u>.

Attributing quotations and direct speech

When we include quotations and direct speech in a piece of writing, we usually include a clause or a phrase introducing or attributing it to the person who wrote it or the character who said it. For example:

In the first scene of Shakespeare's *Twelfth Night*, Duke Orsino says, 'Music is the food of love.'

Notice that a comma has been used to separate the attribution, *Duke Orsino says*, from the quotation itself. It's very common, however, for the attribution to come after the quotation. This is particularly true when it comes to direct speech in works of fiction:

'It's wonderful to see you,' Abigail said, 'and you look so well!'

Notice that there are two commas here. One comes at the end of the first part of the quotation but within the inverted commas. The second comes after the attribution, *Abigail said*, and before the quotation resumes. You can read more about punctuating direct speech in Chapter 15, page 143.

Indicating who or what is being addressed

Very often we use commas to indicate that a clause or a phrase is directed at a particular person, object or group:

Show me your homework please, <u>Tomasz</u>.

Welcome home, <u>my friends</u>.

<u>Miss</u>, can I go to the toilet?

In all of these examples, the comma is separating the name or a description of those being addressed from the words that are actually being said to them. This is another situation where misplaced commas can cause some very serious ambiguities. Imagine a group of children asked a teacher what the staff room was for and she gave this response:

The staff room is where the teachers eat, children.

You may notice that the comma in this example is absolutely essential, and without it the sentence has a very different meaning indeed!

Commas and main clauses

The most common mistake that people make with commas is so widespread that it has its own name: <u>comma splicing</u>. Comma splicing means sticking a comma between two main clauses to separate them. It's the unholy offspring of an education in which children have been taught to see commas merely as 'pauses'. Here are some examples.

Example 1

~~I walked up to the door, I stepped inside.~~

These are both main clauses. If the writer wished, they could place a full stop after the first clause and start a new sentence. Alternatively, they could separate the clauses with a semi-colon or a coordinating conjunction like *and*. However, it is <u>not</u> acceptable in standard English to separate two main clauses with nothing more than a comma. However, it <u>is</u> acceptable to separate the two clauses with a comma *and* a coordinating conjunction:

I walked up to the door, and I stepped inside.

The comma is completely optional in this case but, if the writer opts to include it, they should ensure that the coordinating conjunction is present too.

Example 2

You will sometimes see main clauses separated with a comma if there are more than two of them and they serve as items in a list, e.g.:

He checked his mirrors, he changed gear and he turned the wheel.

These three main clauses are all of equal importance to the meaning of the sentence and, if there were only two of them, the usual conventions would apply when separating them. However, in this example, the three main clauses are items in a list and they have been arranged according to that set of conventions. This is just one more reason why talking about 'grammar rules' is often quite unhelpful.

Teaching ideas

In Key Stage 1, the expectation is that children will know how to use commas to separate items in a list. Using commas to join clauses is introduced in Key Stage 2, as is reflected in these teaching suggestions. For ideas for teaching commas to link subordinate and main clauses, go to either Chapter 9, 'Main and subordinate clauses', page 97, or Chapter 10, 'Types of subordinate clause', page 103. For more ideas about how to teach punctuating direct speech, head to Chapter 15, 'Inverted commas', page 143.

`KS1` I went to the supermarket...

As a teacher, you're probably familiar with the game 'I went to the supermarket'. The children sit in a circle and the first child says, 'I went to the supermarket and I bought an apple.' The next child says, 'I went to the supermarket and I bought an apple and _____', and so on. It's a good test of children's listening skills and their short-term memory. But why not up the ante and use it as a chance to consolidate commas in a list? Instead of just listing the items, get your pupils to say the punctuation, e.g. *'I went to the supermarket and I bought an apple – comma – a book – comma – a pack of colouring pencils AND a tin of tuna.'* You could even get the rest of the class to join in with saying 'comma' so that it is consolidating it for everyone.

`KS1` Add in the commas

Provide pupils with a sentence that includes a list of items but no sentence punctuation. Get them to add in the capital letters, full stop and commas. As you have probably guessed, there are a few of these sentences ready to go on the next page and also available as a worksheet in the online resources!

Sentences

in my suitcase I packed a sunhat pyjamas a t-shirt and a pair of shorts

my hobbies are playing tennis swimming and gymnastics

we are either going to Tenerife Zante or Nice for our holiday this year

when we go swimming we must remember our goggles a towel and a swimming costume

the cat likes to eat sleep and play in the garden

in the holidays I went to the cinema played with my friends watched TV and went to my grandma's house

she can play the piano the flute the violin the harp and the trombone

you can have chocolate crisps or ice cream but not all three

can you go to the shop and buy some milk three apples a packet of crisps and a banana

for Christmas I would like a teddy bear a catapult and some Top Trump cards

at the zoo we saw lions tigers koala bears and meerkats

Add the commas

There is an extract for this activity provided below and also as a printable worksheet in the online resources. The extract uses commas for all of the reasons outlined in this chapter. You could get your class to add the commas to the extract as an initial assessment to find out how much they already know. Alternatively, once you have covered this content with your class, you could get them to add the commas to the text to test their knowledge.

Extract

'OK we're leaving in five minutes Priya' said Mum. Priya sighed. Why did they have to go to stupid Norfolk? All her friends were going to exotic places for their holidays like Dubai Thailand and Canada. Sadly Priya's parents preferred taking holidays in Britain. It wasn't fair. With another heavy sigh she returned to packing her suitcase. So far she had packed: eight different outfits her iPad seven books four cuddly toys and all of her drawing things. What else would she need? Before she'd had a chance to think her mum called up again.

'Priya! Are you ready?'

Priya picked up her case groaning under the weight of it and headed downstairs.

'Mum do we really have to go to Norfolk? I don't even like boats' she pleaded.

'Oh don't be silly Priya. You'll love it once we're there. Now go and find your dad and tell him we're ready to go.'

At that precise moment Priya's dad who had been making last-minute changes to the route appeared in the doorway.

'We've got a bit of a problem' he said gloomily.

UKS2 Ambiguous sentences

Once you're confident that your class are using commas accurately, you can introduce the idea of the Oxford comma. Show them the sentence we discussed earlier in the chapter:

I went to the park with my two dogs, Nick, and Simon.

Can they spot what the two interpretations of that sentence are? Do they understand why the meaning is ambiguous until you add the additional comma? Challenge your pupils to come up with their own ambiguous sentences and share them with the class. If you want to take it even further, you could have a debate about whether, as a class, you are going to adopt the Oxford comma in your written work.

Chapter 14

Semi-colons, colons, brackets, dashes and forward slashes

Chapter overview

Knowing when to use a semi-colon is a bit like knowing how to change a tyre: you won't have to do it very often but you'll feel incredibly smug when you do. In this chapter we will look at:

• The conventions surrounding the use of semi-colons and colons.	LKS2	Pages 136–137
• Using brackets and dashes for parenthesis.	UKS2	Pages 137–139
• The role of the forward slash.	UKS2	Page 139
• Ideas and resources to support teaching of these concepts.	LKS2 UKS2	Pages 140–142

In the previous chapter we looked at the conventions surrounding commas. In this chapter we're going to explore some of the other punctuation you might find in the middle of a sentence.

What you need to know

The conventions around these punctuation marks are shifting all the time. Children are often reluctant to use them and teachers are often reluctant to teach their pupils to use them because those conventions can be vague and ambiguous. However, it's worth getting it right. When your pupils can punctuate their sentences confidently, they will write with greater flair and accuracy.

Semi-colons

Semi-colons are mainly used to separate two main clauses. In these cases, they are an alternative to using a coordinating conjunction such as *and* or *but*.

I'm going to check the weather forecast; I'm not sure what to wear today.

Like all main clauses, both parts of this sentence could stand on their own. Grammatically, it would be perfectly acceptable to put a full-stop after *forecast* and start a new sentence. However, the writer has decided that these two clauses are so closely related that they should probably form one sentence. The semi-colon binds the two clauses together without requiring any additional words to be added.

I don't want to go on my own; will you come with me?

This sentence also contains two main clauses – one a statement and one a question – so closely connected that the writer has decided to merge them into one sentence. Notice that the main clause after the semi-colon does not begin with a capital letter unless the first word is ordinarily capitalised. The semi-colon in the example above could be replaced by the coordinating conjunction *so* but that might feel a little clunky in this relatively short utterance. When to start a new sentence, when to use a coordinating conjunction and when to use a semi-colon is a question of style. Children should be encouraged to experiment with all three techniques and consider their different effects.

As well as separating two main clauses, semi-colons can also be used to separate items in a list. While commas are usually preferred for this purpose, semi-colons can be a useful alternative to avoid confusion when the items being listed contain commas themselves, e.g.:

We have divided you into three teams: Natalie, Chris and Jason are in Team 1; Edith, Karen and Manish are in Team 2; and Ewan, Kelly and Rumaysa are in Team 3.

Essentially, this is a list of lists! To avoid confusion, a semi-colon has been used to separate each list. There is no situation in which anyone is compelled to use a semi-colon. Many respected writers produce entire books that contain no semi-colons at all. However, teaching children how to use them correctly adds to the range of tools they have at their disposal when writing and it will help to eliminate comma splicing from their work.

Colons

Colons serve several functions. Firstly, they can often be found introducing a list or a quotation, e.g.:

Three other countries border Finland: Norway, Sweden and Russia.
As Ludwig Wittgenstein once said: 'If a lion could speak, we would not understand him.'

In both of these examples, the item or items after the colon provide a resolution to what the writer promised before the colon. In a similar way, colons can be used to separate two parts of a sentence where the second part explains or elaborates on the first:

There are two things I won't tolerate around here: selfishness and laziness.

Notice that the abstract nouns after the colon explain and elaborate the sentiment expressed in the main clause. They tell us what the two things are that the writer won't tolerate. The first part of the sentence before the colon is almost always a main clause but the second part can be a single word, a phrase, a subordinate clause or another main clause. Here are some examples:

They now had only one option left: retreat.	One word after the colon
He couldn't believe what he saw: the ghost of his old friend.	Noun phrase after the colon
She knew what she had to do: she must find the key herself.	Main clause after the colon

In all of the examples above, the main clause before the colon sets up an idea that needs resolving or creates a question in the reader's mind that needs answering. The words after the colon resolve those ideas and answer those questions. As with semi-colons, the word after a colon does not need to start with a capital letter unless it would ordinarily. Sometimes a colon will be used to explain the word or phrase at the end of the main clause before it, especially when the writer suspects that the reader might not understand it. For example:

On 27 April each year, people in the Netherlands celebrate the *Koningsdag*: the Dutch king's official birthday.

Brackets

In the last chapter, we looked at how commas can be used for parenthesis, clarifying or naming something that has just been said. Brackets provide a less subtle form of parenthesis, which completely interrupts the grammatical structure of the sentence:

The BBC (British Broadcasting Corporation) was founded in 1922.

The words in brackets in this sentence are clearly understood to offer the full name represented by the abbreviation *BBC*. It serves no other grammatical function in the sentence, which would still make perfect sense if the parenthesised words were removed.

People often get somewhat confused about punctuation after brackets. A good general tip here is to ask yourself: does the punctuation apply to the whole sentence or just the section in brackets? Consider this example:

There are two ways to get out of the building: out of the window (not a good idea!) or down the stairs.

In this example, the exclamation mark is specific to the remark *not a good idea*; therefore, it sits inside the brackets alongside it. Contrast it with this example:

Giving the ball back to Fred (it was his), I went back inside.

In this example, the comma is separating the entire fronted subordinate clause, not just the words in brackets, from the main clause; therefore, it sits outside the brackets. Sometimes you may even find you need two punctuation marks, one either side of the closing bracket:

I decided to stop worrying about it; after all, it was just a dream (wasn't it?).

In this example, the question mark applies only to the brief interrogative clause in brackets, whereas the full stop brings the entire sentence to an end. Therefore the question mark sits inside the brackets but the full stop sits outside.

When reading newspaper articles with older children, you may find you encounter square brackets, as these are becoming increasingly common. They are particularly useful for removing ambiguity in quotations. Look at this sentence:

The Prime Minister criticised the Leader of the Opposition during a joint press conference with the President of France, saying, 'He clearly hasn't thought this through.'

If this were said at a time when the Leader of the Opposition and the Prime Minister were both men, there would be room for confusion here. Does *he* refer to the Leader of the Opposition or the President? Any potential confusion can be removed by replacing the ambiguous pronoun with clearer language, punctuated by square brackets:

The Prime Minister criticised the Leader of the Opposition during a joint press conference with the President of France, saying, '[The Leader of the Opposition] clearly hasn't thought this through.'

The square brackets indicate to the reader that its contents do not reflect the actual words uttered but they refer to the same thing.

Dashes

Dashes, also known as 'en dashes', are an extremely versatile and very useful punctuation mark. In appearance, an en dash is slightly longer than a hyphen and serves a different purpose. Dashes can be used as an alternative to semi-colons, colons or the three dots of an ellipsis. Have a look at these examples:

This is going to be a wonderful holiday; I can't wait to get going.
This is going to be a wonderful holiday – I can't wait to get going.

There are two problems with my new oven: it's too large and it's too loud.
There are two problems with my new oven – it's too large and it's too loud.

There's nothing that can possibly go wrong now… I hope.
There's nothing that can possibly go wrong now – I hope.

In each of these examples, the dash is merely an optional alternative to another punctuation mark. No two ways of writing a sentence ever have *exactly* the same effect and it would be interesting to discuss with your pupils how the dash alters their interpretation of each sentence.

The dash is particularly useful when you've already used a semi-colon or a colon in your sentence and you feel that it would look strange to use another one. For example:

She'd never missed a penalty yet and she wasn't planning to start now; she struck the ball cleanly and the goalkeeper went the wrong way – the crowd was already on their feet as the ball hit the back of the net.

The writer in this example has taken the decision that these clauses narrate dramatic, action-packed events that would be slowed down if they were split into shorter sentences. The coordinating conjunction *and* has already been used to separate two main clauses twice, and including two semi-colons in the same sentence to separate main clauses would look a little odd. In this instance, the dash is a handy alternative.

The double dash

A pair of en dashes (or a double dash) can be used in the same way that commas and brackets can be used for parenthesis. Have a look at the following examples:

Hippos – despite their enormous size – can run at 19 mph.

And yet, when the house had finally sold – nearly ten months after it went on the market – the Brown family decided they no longer wanted to move, leaving the estate agent in a tricky situation.

The staggering cost – up 57 per cent since 2015 – makes this a luxury item for most families.

These sentences would still make sense if you removed the words in between the dashes. The parenthesis provides additional information for the reader. The use of dashes is considered more intrusive than using commas; use dashes if you want to draw the reader's attention to the extra information.

The forward slash

The forward slash is a common enough sight in modern English to merit a mention here. It serves as a disjunction – that is to say, it can stand in for the word 'or', e.g.:

Britain held an in/out referendum on its membership of the EU.

Despite its best efforts to prove otherwise over the last 50 years, Britain cannot be both in and out of the EU. There is therefore a disjunction between the two ideas, expressed in this sentence with a forward slash.

Teaching ideas

All of the punctuation marks covered in this chapter are from the Key Stage 2 curriculum (which is why there aren't any suggested activities for Key Stage 1!).

Add the semi-colon

Provide your pupils with a variety of compound sentences and ask them to add the semi-colons. To increase the level of challenge, you may want to mix in a few complex sentences that don't require a semi-colon to see whether they can decipher between the two. You can use the examples below, also provided as a worksheet in the online resources, as a starting point.

> Our aim was to score three goals we only scored one goal.
> Call me in the morning I will give you my answer then.
> The children were exhausted the party had gone on until midnight.
> Tim loved history Zoe loved English.
> My birthday is in November Frank's birthday is in May.
> I can highly recommend that restaurant the service and food are exceptional.
> My hair is wet I forgot my umbrella.
> The cat went to sleep it had been a long day.

Add the brackets

This is a simple exercise for assessing your class's understanding of where brackets go in a sentence. Use the sentences below (also available as a printable worksheet in the online resources). Read them aloud as a class and ask your class to find the part of the sentence that requires brackets.

> The thief knew he couldn't get into this particular safe an HVSX2019 safe without using his tools.
> King Louis XIV sometimes known as the Sun King ruled France in the 17th century.
> Clare couldn't work out how she a geographer had got lost.
> The doctor did an MRI magnetic resonance imaging scan.
> We are vegetarian we don't eat meat.
> They went to the zoo with Maya's mum Meera.
> The majority of my class 92 per cent are going to the local secondary school.
> The Year 6 teacher Miss Campbell also teaches Spanish.

Add the punctuation

LKS2

UKS2

By this point, your class have covered all of the punctuation in the primary curriculum (hurrah!). It's time to see how they use it. Give them a copy of the modelled text below (also available as a worksheet in the online resources) and ask them to punctuate it using relevant punctuation. It's likely that each of them will choose to punctuate it slightly differently. Once they have finished, get your pupils to swap their work with a partner and compare their decisions – what effect has this had on the meaning of the text?

Modelled text

It wasnt an ordinary friendship Zog was an alien Sophia was a six-year-old human Zog had dark blue skin Sophia had pale skin they had been friends for two years ever since Zogs spaceship had crashed into Sophias garden without thinking Sophia had rushed out to find out what was going on there was lots of smoke a strange buzzing sound and there in the middle of the wreckage was a little blue alien Zog

Hello said Sophia giving a shy wave what is your name I is Zog from the planet Jedanton who are you

I am Sophia from Planet Earth this is my home would you like to come in for tea

Cautiously Zog followed Sophia into the house to the kitchen

What would you like to eat she asked her guest

Zog likes Gloonburgers

Oh I dont think we have any of those what about a cheese sandwich

Zog thinks that is OK

Sophia made two cheese sandwiches and cut them into triangles just like her mum had taught her

Zog sat on the floor Sophia sat at the table

Zog you can come and sit with me up here if you would like

They ate their sandwiches in a comfortable silence you would not necessarily expect between an alien and a small girl and so began a lifelong friendship full of amazing adventures

---

The play's the thing

LKS2

UKS2

Play scripts are a fantastic tool for teaching the importance of punctuation. The punctuation in a play script is essential as it tells the actors how and when to deliver their lines. Explore a few scripts with your class (why not do this when you are preparing them for a performance or class assembly so that you can use the scripts they already have?). Then get your pupils to convert one of their favourite stories into a play script. Encourage them to think carefully about the punctuation they use. Once they're happy with their script, they can get into small groups and have a go at performing one another's plays. This will give them a sense of how effective the punctuation they have included is at helping the actors deliver their lines.

 ## Dash or double dash?

 Have a look at the sentences below. Some require a single dash and others a double dash. Challenge your pupils to complete the sentences with the dashes. There is a worksheet available in the online resources for this activity.

> My sister Alisha likes to eat cheese.
> There has been a power cut at school and we've all been sent home early what a pity!
> We made pie apple and blackberry for dinner.
> Finally after months of training the day of the marathon arrived.
> 'You you IDIOT!' she shouted.
> My cat Bubbles is a long-haired moggy.
> She got home, put the kettle on and sat down then she remembered.
> We were home safe and sound or so we thought!

Chapter 15

Inverted commas

Chapter overview

Here's the bad news: there are a number of conventions to follow when using inverted commas. The good news is there aren't nearly as many conventions as you think there are. In this chapter we will look at:

• The differences between direct and reported speech.	LKS2	Page 144
• The conventions for setting out direct speech.	LKS2	Pages 144–146
• The conventions for using inverted commas to embed quotations or imply 'air quotes'.	UKS2	Pages 146–147
• Ideas and resources to support teaching of these concepts.	LKS2 UKS2	Pages 147–149

Whoever first started teaching children about 'speech marks' and 'quotation marks' was doubtless well intentioned, hoping to give their pupils a simpler name for <u>inverted commas</u> that would make their purpose clearer. The effect has been far from simple, causing generations of children and adults to imagine they were breaking a plethora of strict rules where in fact none existed. Children will still ask what the difference is between speech marks and quotation marks (there isn't one) or when it is 'correct' to use one or two inverted commas to open and close speech (it doesn't matter).

Inverted commas is a grammatical term used to describe commas turned upside down at the top of the line (i.e. inverted from the usual position of a comma). They are used to indicate that the words within them were said by someone other than the author. You can use one or two at each end depending on your preference – different authors and publishers have different house approaches, none of which is more 'correct' than any other.

However, there are still a few other issues surrounding the use of inverted commas that can cause problems, so let's take a closer look.

What you need to know

Any teacher who has ever tried to read a child's description of a conversation between two or more characters with no speech punctuation whatsoever will know exactly how essential inverted commas can be to aiding the reader's understanding. They will also know that endless dialogue is rarely the most interesting way to tell a story. Let's consider the ways in which we can help our pupils to use speech accurately and sparingly to good effect.

Direct and reported speech

When teaching children to write stories, it's a good idea to explain the difference between direct speech and reported speech. Direct speech involves writing down exactly what a character said using inverted commas. Reported speech, on the other hand, involves indirectly reporting the meaning of what was said. Consider these two sentences:

'To get to the station,' Margaret said to Wilbur, 'you must carry on down Park Road and take the second road on the right.'
Margaret directed Wilbur to the station.

In the first of these examples, you will notice that the reader is given the exact words Margaret used. In the second, we simply know that Margaret gave Wilbur the directions. Once they've learnt to punctuate speech, you will often find that primary school children's stories become leaden with dull and narratively inconsequential dialogue along the following lines:

'Hi,' Daisy said, 'how are you?'
'I'm fine, thanks,' Doris replied. 'How are you?'
'I'm good, thanks,' Daisy answered. 'Do you want to play tennis?'
'Yes, that would be lovely. Thank you.'

Dialogue like this adds nothing to the plot of any story. The exact words used in such an exchange don't matter and won't have any discernible effect on the reader other than to bore them. It's a good idea, therefore, to encourage children to replace exchanges like this with some succinct reported speech:

After greeting one another warmly, Daisy and Doris decided to play tennis.

However, sometimes the precise words do matter. The tone and vocabulary used by a character are one of the ways in which a reader gets to know them, and sometimes their words have a hidden meaning that becomes clearer later in the story. Very often, therefore, direct speech is necessary and children will need to learn the fairly complex conventions for setting it out.

Conventions for writing direct speech

We've divided the conventions for setting out direct speech into five sections. These are in no particular order.

Convention 1

When writing direct speech, inverted commas are placed at either end of what is said by the character and nothing else. It doesn't matter whether they're '66s and 99s' or just little dashes. It doesn't matter whether there are one or two of them. Many teachers encourage children to use two as they are less likely to be mistaken for commas on the line above.

'I'm somewhat disappointed,' Mr Noakes announced.

"I'm somewhat disappointed," Mr Noakes announced.

The author or narrator in this example is saying the words *Mr Noakes announced* whereas Mr Noakes himself is saying the words *I'm somewhat disappointed*.

Convention 2

A clause attributing the speech to a particular character (telling the reader who is saying it) can be placed before, after or in the middle of the direct speech:

Peter asked, 'Who are you and why are you here?'

'Who are you and why are you here?' Peter asked.

'Who are you?' Peter asked. 'And why are you here?'

Notice the capital 'A' following the clause that attributes the speech to Peter. This is because it forms the beginning of a new sentence.

When writing longer sections of dialogue, reporting clauses can be dropped once it has been made clear to the reader who is saying what.

Convention 3

When adding a clause to direct speech to attribute it to a character, the subject and verb can be swapped around, but not if the subject is a pronoun:

'Good morning, Mrs Briggs,' the children said.

'Good morning, Mrs Briggs,' said the children.

'Good morning, Mrs Briggs,' they said.

~~'Good morning, Mrs Briggs,' said they.~~

The first three examples above are all acceptable forms, whereas the fourth is not. In most English clauses, the subject precedes the verb. We have the option of reversing them when reporting speech. However, to do so would look very odd indeed if the subject were a pronoun, as in the fourth example. There are archaic examples (e.g. *'I am the Lord of the Dance,' said he*) but it isn't generally done in modern English.

Convention 4

Direct speech always ends with a comma, a full stop, an exclamation mark, a question mark or an ellipsis. This punctuation <u>almost always sits inside the inverted commas</u>. The clause attributing speech to a particular character is often separated from the direct speech by a comma, although you will also see authors employing variations to this convention. Common exceptions include cases where the direct speech ends with a question mark, an exclamation mark or an ellipsis:

'Where are we going?' David asked. 'We've been travelling for ages.'

'Scotland,' the driver replied. 'Didn't anyone tell you?'

Convention 5

You start a new line for a new speaker.

'Name?' the officer demanded.

'Louise Barnes,' Jill lied, nervously.

You'll often find that authors start a new line not just when the new speaker starts talking, but as soon as they become the subject of the sentence:

Karim wandered across the playground and saw Micah on the climbing frame. 'Boo!' he shouted.

Micah almost lost his footing. 'You scared me!'

Notice that in this case the author has started a new line one sentence before the new speaker says anything. This is because attention has now switched to Micah and it makes it obvious, even without an attribution, that the words *You scared me* were uttered by him.

Quotations

The grammatical conventions for including quotations in a piece of non-fiction writing are similar to those of setting out direct speech. However, the ways in which quotations are attributed to the people who wrote or said them can be quite different to those employed in fiction. For a start, attributing a quotation to its author in the middle or at the end is rare. A quotation is much more likely to be preceded by a short phrase or clause ending in a colon, rather than the comma that would be more normal in fictional dialogue, e.g.:

As J. S. Mill once said: 'He who knows only his own side of the case knows little of that.'

According to Lady Gaga: 'Love is like a brick.'

Another common way of citing quotations is by placing them as the logical grammatical continuation of a sentence, e.g.:

Winston Churchill, famously, was adamant that Britain would 'never surrender'.

Notice that this sentence would still make grammatical sense without the inverted commas. The words uttered by Churchill are 'sewn into the grammatical fabric' of the whole sentence.

Air quotes

The other instance in which inverted commas are commonly used is to draw attention to a word or phrase that may seem strange, unfamiliar or out of place in a sentence. These are the occasions when, in conversation, we might make Dr Evil-style 'air quotes' with our fingers as we speak:

I invented this myself. I call it 'the Mind Machine'.

In this sentence, the speaker is coining a new name for something, and the hitherto unfamiliar phrase is highlighted with inverted commas.

Things went from bad to worse when we arrived at our 'hotel'.

In this sentence, we can see that the word *hotel* has been placed in inverted commas. The implication is that the hotel was so bad, it's misleading to even call it a hotel at all.

Teaching ideas

According to the National Curriculum, inverted commas are introduced in Year 3 so, for this reason, all of the following activities are aimed at Key Stage 2 pupils.

Identifying direct speech

The first step in writing direct speech is being able to identify direct speech. Read a short extract of a story with your class and provide them with a blank comic strip template (we've supplied one in the online resources). Ask them to create a comic strip of the extract, using speech bubbles for the direct speech.

Texts into dialogue

This activity always goes down well with a class and gives you a chance to assess whether or not they understand the conventions for setting out direct speech. Provide your class with a screenshot of text messages between two people. Use https://ifaketextmessage.com to create them rather than showing messages from your own phone... You might want to write text messages from characters from the book you are reading in class or from famous figures in science or history. The following example is an exchange between Hermione and Harry Potter. The task is to convert the texts into a dialogue using full speech punctuation. To extend the task, get your class to imagine the rest of the conversation and continue their dialogue.

LKS2 Who said that?

UKS2 Below, there is a table with two columns: one side is a list of famous people from throughout history; the other side shows famous quotations. The task is to match the quotation to the famous person (this might require a bit of research) and write the answers in full sentences, using inverted commas, e.g.:

Winnie the Pooh said, 'You're braver than you believe and stronger and smarter than you think.'

There is a printable worksheet for this activity in the online resources.

Neil Armstrong	God bless us, everyone.
Muhammad Ali	One book, one pen, one child, and one teacher can change the world.
Rosa Parks	We shall fight on the beaches.
Buzz Lightyear	Float like a butterfly, sting like a bee.

Winston Churchill	That's one small step for a man, one giant leap for mankind.
Malala Yousafzai	You have brains in your head. You have feet in your shoes. You can steer yourself any direction you choose.
Tiny Tim	To infinity... and beyond!
Dr. Seuss	All I was doing was trying to get home from work.
Audrey Hepburn	Nothing in life is to be feared; it is only to be understood. Now is the time to understand more, so that we may fear less.
Marie Curie	Nothing is impossible; the word itself says 'I'm possible'!

Convert a play script

We've already discussed in Chapter 14, page 141, how useful play scripts can be for teaching punctuation. For this activity, start by getting the class to perform a play script. Then set the task of converting a play script into a dialogue using full speech punctuation. Encourage your class to think about how to incorporate the stage directions into their work.

Add the dialogue

Watch a short wordless animation, e.g. Pixar's 'For the Birds' at www.youtube.com/watch?v=WjoDEQqyTig. Get your class to act out the story in small groups, adding their own dialogue, and watch each group's performance. Then get each child to write their own dialogue to go with the animation. The Literacy Shed is a fantastic place for short videos if you're stuck.

Part Three

Writing with flair

Chapter 16

Moods and voices

Chapter overview

In this chapter we're going to cover four moods that we think are really useful to know about and one that we think is a bit daft. We will be looking at:

• The five 'moods' commonly used in standard English.	UKS2	Pages 154–156
• The difference between the active and passive voice.	UKS2	Pages 156–157
• Ideas and resources to support teaching of these concepts.	UKS2	Pages 157–159

The National Curriculum requires that we teach children about the differences between statements, questions and commands, also known as the <u>indicative,</u> <u>interrogative</u> and <u>impera-tive moods</u> respectively. That seems pretty sensible to us. The National Curriculum also requires that we teach children to use and identify the <u>subjunctive mood</u>. This seems pretty silly to us. However, since we're required to teach four of the five 'moods' commonly used in modern standard English, we figured we might as well throw in the fifth one, the <u>conditional mood</u>, for free. Exciting, right?

As well as getting moody, this chapter will tackle the difference between the <u>active</u> and <u>passive voices.</u> Learning and then teaching all these technical terms can get a bit tedious but hopefully you can use the information and ideas in this chapter to give your pupils some subtle tricks to make their writing more sophisticated.

What you need to know

Unfortunately, the word 'mood' starts to look really weird when you use it a lot and that's exactly what we're going to be doing. We should probably explain that a grammatical mood doesn't really have anything to do with the everyday definition of the word, and none of the moods we'll be looking at should make you cry – although that may be the effect this stuff has on some Year 6 teachers when they see it on the syllabus.

The indicative mood, *aka* statements

The good news is that the indicative mood is nice and easy. Indicative clauses are statements. They are clauses that, quite simply, tell us something. They inform the reader that *a* is *b* or that *c* does *d*:

Mary Ann Evans published her books using the pen name 'George Eliot'.

Bad things happen to good people.

Characters played by Sean Bean in films and TV shows almost always die.

Each of these sentences is an assertion, a declaration, a proposition. Each expresses a fact or a belief. It states that a particular state of affairs is the case.

The interrogative mood, *aka* questions

We've encountered interrogatives a few times already as we've woven our way through the wonders of English grammar. Interrogative clauses ask questions and they tend to end, reassuringly if somewhat predictably, with a question mark. Some interrogative clauses are headed by relative pronouns and these usually pose open questions:

Where is Sarah Connor?

Who stole my cheese?

Some interrogative clauses, meanwhile, pose binary questions or closed yes/no questions. These tend to start with a suitable form of the verbs *to have*, *to do* or *to be* or with a modal verb:

Is this the real life or is this just fantasy?

Do you think this is a good idea?

Should you be eating that?

Have you seen Sarah Connor?

Some indicative clauses can be turned into interrogative clauses simply by adding a question mark:

This is your idea of fun?

I don't suppose you're feeling hungry?

The imperative mood, *aka* commands

Some teachers like to teach children how to write imperatives by talking about 'bossy verbs' and this is a pretty good way to introduce the idea to young children:

Mix together 300g of flour, 200g of caster sugar and two eggs.

Stop it.

Take your marks, get set – go!

While we're teaching children about imperatives, it's also a good opportunity to talk about manners, if the Department for Education will allow us a couple of minutes of such woolly, liberal frivolity within their austere diet of rigorous, undiluted grammar. Imperatives are a big part of a child's world. Children find themselves on the receiving end of them a lot and, as a result, they tend to use them more than most adults too. It's probably a good idea to teach children that, to help everyone in our society get along, we tend to turn our imperatives into interrogatives or indicatives:

Would you mind coming over here for a moment?

I'd prefer it if you didn't do that.

The subjunctive mood, *aka* Mr Gove's school days

The subjunctive is a formal and somewhat old-fashioned mood used to describe *desired outcomes*. Typically, you'll see a verb early on in the sentence that deals with <u>someone trying to get someone else to do something</u> – *ask, demand, insist, recommend, require, suggest,* etc. This is then followed by a subjunctive clause explaining what precisely it is that someone was trying to get someone else to do. The subjunctive clause contains the base form of its main verb (the infinitive minus the word *to* – see Appendix 4, page 185, for more on infinitives). Confused? Well, of course you are. Let's look at some examples and hopefully you'll start to understand:

The alderman's wife insisted that Mrs Parker-Daniels <u>attend</u> supper at their residence.

I humbly request that Her Majesty <u>grant</u> an audience to a faithful subject.

I suggested that my mate Chris <u>stop</u> watching *Love Island*.

Notice that the verb in the main clause in each case is in the base form regardless of tense and person – not an *-s* or an *-ed* ending in sight. The modern and informal context of the third sentence looks rather incongruous and quite funny after the highbrow tone of the first two sentences. However, it's there to make a serious point, which is that the subjunctive is becoming increasingly obsolete. These sentences would all be completely acceptable if their writers had stuck to the indicative mood:

The alderman's wife insisted that Mrs Parker-Daniels <u>attended</u> supper at their residence.

I humbly request that Her Majesty <u>grants</u> an audience to a faithful subject.

I suggested that my mate Chris <u>stopped</u> watching *Love Island*.

The subjunctive is never mandatory but, if they do learn about it, children will be able to adopt a more formal register when writing in role as historical characters, which could result in some interesting work. Apart from one extra mark on the grammar test (in some years but not others), that's about all we can promise!

The conditional mood, *aka* hypothetical situations

Conditional clauses are used to introduce hypothetical scenarios and usually begin with the word *if*. However, they can also be linked to the main clause with other subordinating conjunctions such as *unless* or *as soon as*. Conditional clauses are somewhat unusual as they will often (though not always) use past or present tense verbs to introduce hypothetical events in the future:

<u>If I won the lottery</u>, I'd give half to charity and spend the rest on myself.

<u>I'm getting a job as soon as</u> I've finished my exams.

I think I can do this <u>if I try my best</u>.

<u>Unless you help her</u>, she's in real trouble.

It's worth spending a bit of time on conditionals with children as they can be prone to using unacceptable forms like this:

~~If I will win the lottery, I will buy a big car.~~

Whether the poor grammar or the vulgar materialism upsets you more is your own business, but a mistake like this is completely understandable as both the hypothetical lottery win and the hypothetical car would be events in the future.

The active and passive voice

Almost all the sentences we've included as illustrative examples in this book so far have been written in the active voice. That is to say, the subject of the sentence is the *doer of the verb*:

J. K. Rowling wrote the Harry Potter books.

Wrote is the verb in this sentence. *J. K. Rowling* is the subject of the sentence, for it was she who did the writing. However, this sentence can be swapped around:

The Harry Potter books were written by J. K. Rowling.

This is now written in the passive voice. *Were written* is now the verb phrase and *The Harry Potter books* are now the subject, for it is they that were written. Apologies to our fellow Bloomsbury author: Ms Rowling herself has now been exiled to a prepositional phrase at the end of the sentence.

Sentences are written in the passive voice when the author wishes to give prominence to *the person or thing upon whom the verb was enacted*, rather than *the person or thing who enacted the verb*. Consider these two sentences:

A violent criminal attacked an innocent pensioner.   Active

An innocent pensioner was attacked by a violent criminal.   Passive

You will often see the passive voice used in news reports about unpleasant incidents like this for a very good reason. Using the active in this case makes the violent criminal the star of the show – the main character in the story. So, even though it was the violent criminal who *attacked*, the writer in the second sentence has switched to the passive and made the innocent pensioner the subject of the sentence – the person who *was attacked*. The pensioner is now the centre of the story – the person around whom the reader's interest and sympathy revolves. Here is another example:

We resolved the matter.   Active

The matter has been resolved.   Passive

Sometimes, switching from active to passive can <u>depersonalise</u> an issue. In this case, perhaps the writer wishes to be modest and avoid looking like they're trying to take all the credit for resolving the matter. Alternatively, perhaps, the manner in which the matter was resolved was somewhat controversial, and using the passive voice distances those responsible from the decision they've taken. Perhaps, for whatever reason, the writer simply feels that the slightly more formal tone of the passive version is more appropriate.

A clause written in the passive voice always involves some form of the verb *to be* alongside the main verb. Precisely which form of the verb *to be* is used depends on the person and tense involved. A lot of academic writing, from history essays to reports of scientific investigations, sounds considerably more sophisticated when the passive voice is employed confidently:

One of the plants <u>was placed</u> in a dark room, with the other <u>being left</u> in direct sunlight.

Incontrovertible evidence as to the fate of the princes has yet <u>to be discovered</u>.

A colour change <u>was observed</u> as the beaker was heated.

Caesar's own accounts of his military campaigns <u>should be treated</u> with some scepticism.

Teaching ideas

Everything covered in this chapter is in the curriculum for upper Key Stage 2, so all of these activities have been planned with Year 5 and 6 pupils in mind. There are further teaching ideas for the different moods in Chapter 4, page 51 – make this your first port of call.

Write election speeches   `UKS2`

Hone your pupils' understanding of the conditional by getting them to write election speeches under the title 'If I were your prime minister…'. Discuss how the conditional mood lends itself to more formal writing, e.g. speeches, formal letters, etc. As each child delivers their speech, ask the rest of the class to listen out for examples of the conditional mood.

UKS2 Identify the mood

Read through the extract below and explain that it contains a number of examples of the moods the pupils have learnt about. Agree on a key as a class, using different colours for the interrogative, subjunctive, etc., and get your pupils to highlight the different moods they can find in the text. There is a digital version of this text in the online resources to avoid you typing it out.

Extract

'Kirsty Phillips, sit down in your chair,' said the teacher sternly. Kirsty rolled her eyes but did as she was told. She caught her friend Zainab's eye and smiled at her.

'OK, 9S, listen carefully as I'm going to explain the summer project.' There was a heavy groan from the class.

'Next year you will start studying for your history GCSE. In preparation, we would like you to do some research about the Russian Revolution. Now, it does not have to be extensive – just a couple of sides of A4 with the key details, events, dates and figures. Do you understand?'

'Why do we have to do homework in the holidays, Miss?' Kirsty called out.

'Well Kirsty, we believe it is good to keep your brain ticking over during the summer. Six weeks is a long time. We wouldn't want you to undo your good work from this year, would we?'

Kirsty shrugged. 'If I were in charge, I would make a rule that children could NEVER have homework,' she replied.

'Well, work hard, do your homework, pass your exams, go to university and then you CAN be in charge,' the teacher replied.

'Ha. As if! I'm getting a job as soon as I've finished my exams. I am out of here.'

'Stop being silly, Kirsty.'

UKS2 Convert active into passive

It's likely your pupils will be more confident about writing in the active rather than the passive. Give them the following sentences written in the active voice and challenge them to rewrite them in the passive. There is a worksheet that you can use for this activity in the online resources.

The boy threw the ball.
The children watered the plants.
Boris Johnson made the speech.
The earthquake destroyed the whole city.
The tiger's roar broke the silence in the jungle.
George drinks four litres of water every day.
David Walliams wrote *Gangsta Granny*.
The frogs inhabited the pond.
The baby scribbled on the wall.

Simon Says

UKS2

Get your class practising using the imperative mood with a game of Simon Says. In this game, the person who is 'Simon' uses the imperative mood to give instructions to the rest of the class, e.g. 'Put your hands on your head.' You can play this game as a whole-class activity, with alternating pupils playing Simon.

Chapter 17

Structuring whole texts

Chapter overview

This book would have been much harder to read if we hadn't used a number of the structuring devices covered in this chapter. We will be looking at:

• The conventions for dividing writing into paragraphs.	LKS2	Page 162
• How to include sub-headings, lists and bullet points.	LKS2	Pages 162–163
• Using cohesive devices to tie whole texts together.	UKS2	Pages 163–164
• Using different registers and maintaining a consistent register across a piece of writing.	UKS2	Pages 164–165
• Ideas and resources to support teaching of these concepts.	UKS2	Pages 165–169

In the first chapter of this book, we looked at how individual words are constructed. Since then, our main focus has been on constructing clauses and sentences to convey meaning. This chapter is going to zoom out again and consider some of the grammatical questions that arise when we write an entire text. We're going to consider paragraphs and other ways of breaking up the parts of a text and yes, we will be discussing that old favourite among grammatical non-issues: how to punctuate bullet points. We'll then be exploring how cohesive devices, registers and discourse markers can enable us to create texts that convey meaning in an appropriately engaging way.

What you need to know

Most of what you need to know in this chapter is that you don't need to know anything! That is to say, the 'rules' you think you're breaking most of the time probably don't really exist.

Paragraphs

'Each paragraph is about a different thing.' That's more or less what we say, right? And, to be honest, it's about right. A paragraph is a series of sentences about a particular topic, theme, event, stage, incident or idea. The only problem is that each sentence, each phrase and sometimes each word can be about a different thing, so what sort of difference is it that determines when a new paragraph is needed? The answer, perhaps somewhat unhelpfully, is that it is up to you, and the decision you make signals to your reader how you think the content you're delivering is best broken down into more manageable chunks.

When writing non-fiction, there's usually a way to divide your text up by topic. So, for example, the paragraph before this one introduced the topic of paragraphs generally and this one is specifically about how to divide up paragraphs when writing non-fiction. When laying out an argument for a point of view, you might want to start a new paragraph for each of your reasons or pieces of evidence. When reporting on a football match, you might want to try to divide the game into rough stages to split up your paragraphs – the context in which the game was played; how Team A started dominant and took a two-goal lead; how Team B came back into the game with two goals of their own either side of half-time; and finally the drama at the final whistle after Team A scored a dodgy penalty to win the match with the last kick of the game. It's up to you – the important thing is that you divide your writing up in such a way that it becomes clearer and more accessible for your reader.

When writing fiction, you have similar decisions to make. Most authors will start a new paragraph when the action moves to another place or a later time. If a lengthy conversation between two characters about a particular issue comes to an end and they turn their attention to something else, that may also signal the end of a paragraph. Many authors will include single paragraphs that serve particular purposes, e.g. a description of a setting. G. R. R. Martin, the author of *Game of Thrones*, will often include an entire paragraph whenever a feast takes place in his stories that describes in meticulous detail the various dishes adorning the table. Then, of course, some fiction authors don't use paragraphs at all. Once again, it's up to the writer to decide how they want to package their content for the reader.

So, how do we divide up paragraphs? Should we skip a line or simply move to the next line? Once again, it's up to you. Do you always have to indent the start of a new paragraph and by how much? Honest answer: who cares? Just make sure it's obvious to the reader where one paragraph ends and another begins.

Sub-headings, lists and bullet points

The rules about sub-headings, lists and bullet points are as follows:

- Use sub-headings if you think they will help your reader to follow the text.
- Use lists and bullet points if you think they will help your reader to follow the text.
- Otherwise, do whatever you want.

Is the full stop compulsory at the end of each bullet point? No. Is the capital letter at the start of each bullet point compulsory? No. Do differently shaped bullet points mean different things? No.

Like hyphens and inverted commas, bullet points cause many people to imagine there is a set of very specific rules that everyone else in the world knows but, for some reason, they were never told about. There isn't. So relax. Let's move on.

Cohesion

<u>Cohesion</u> in everyday English means sticking together, working together, getting along – that kind of thing. In grammar its meaning is much the same: it describes the way in which different clauses and phrases are made to *feel* as though they are all part of the same text. You could call this a sense of the text *flowing*. This is achieved through various <u>cohesive devices</u>.

Pronouns and determiners

One common and very simple cohesive device is to use pronouns and determiners to draw relationships and connections across sentences:

My grandfather served in North Africa during the Second World War. Most of our families contain extraordinary stories if we dig deep enough. <u>He</u> didn't talk about <u>it</u> very much but he must have seen some extraordinary things.

The final sentence contains the pronoun *he* twice and the pronoun *it* once. Reading this passage, you immediately know that *he* refers to *my grandfather* and *it* refers to *his service in North Africa,* even though neither has been mentioned since two sentences previously. The pronouns avoid needless repetition of the same words but subtly draw our understanding of different sentences together without making it sound unnatural.

Adverbials

Another common way to create cohesion in a text is through our use of adverbials:

<u>At nine o'clock,</u> the bell rang and we went into class. I immediately sat down with Serena and started talking to her about my idea for a school radio station. I didn't get to hear what she thought of my plan because Mr Scott called for silence so he could take the register. <u>Two hours later,</u> I was finally able to speak to her again.

In this passage, we know roughly what time the writer was able to speak to Serena again – about 11 o'clock – because of the cohesion created by the two underlined adverbials. Even though they are several sentences apart, they help us to understand the whole text as one cohesive, flowing narrative. We often use time or sequential adverbials (*to begin with, next, after that* or *firstly, secondly, finally*) to achieve the same goal.

Repetition and substitution

**Captain Baxter had sailed all over the world and no one knew more about ships.
'What about the Barracuda?' I suggested. 'I'm sure we'd be allowed to borrow it.'
'The Barracuda is a rotting pile of junk,' the old seafarer replied.**

This extract uses two very common cohesive devices to help the lines of dialogue flow into one another: repetition and substitution. The repetition of the name *Barracuda* reassures the reader that the conversation is flowing logically, and authors need to do this a lot to hold the trust and attention of their audience. This is why most works of fiction will continually refer back to the same characters and objects and, without wishing to sound unkind, a lack of this sort of cohesion is often the reason why many stories written by children can seem a bit disjointed and unengaging. However, it's also off-putting for the reader if they keep seeing the same name or phrase used again and again. That's why, in the example above, the term *the old seafarer* has been used to describe *Captain Baxter* in the last line. As well as making the extract more varied and more interesting, it reinforces what we've already learnt about the character in the first line.

Registers

Register is the grammatical term for the *tone* of a piece of writing. The most important point to get across to children is that more formal registers are needed in some cases than others. The differences in language that contribute to differences in register are very subtle, and teaching them explicitly isn't always easy, but there are some specifics we can draw our pupils' attention to:

He's annoying and his idea is terrible.

His manner can be somewhat alienating and his proposal could be significantly improved.

As an experienced reader in the English language, you are doubtless able to identify that these two sentences express similar sentiments in different registers; the first is more informal and cavalier while the second is more formal and cautious. The first thing children will notice is that formal registers are more likely to contain 'big words' and this is often true, but there are more important features of a formal register for them to notice:

1. Less personal. Notice the subtle difference between the word *idea* and the word *pro-posal*. An idea is in someone's mind whereas a proposal is something out in the world. Criticising someone's idea therefore sounds a little bit more like a personal dig than criticising their proposal. When writing formally, we try to find less personal ways to talk about personal and potentially sensitive issues. You might say two people are *acquainted* rather than saying they *know each other*, for example, or you might describe someone's *emotions* or *feelings* about an issue as their *reaction*.

2. Greater prevalence of the passive voice. In the first example above, both clauses are written in the active voice, whereas both clauses in the second example are written in

the passive voice. This depersonalises the issues being discussed, making them appear more measured and objective.

3. <u>Objective rather than subjective terms.</u> Saying that someone is *annoying* is subjective and very personal – it sounds like an opinion rather than a fact. However, describing their *manner* as *alienating* sounds far less personal and far more objective. It suggests that, without any personal feelings on the matter, the writer has observed the effect of the person's manner on other people.

4. <u>Use of euphemisms.</u> The term *could be significantly improved* is a euphemism (a more polite way of saying something uncomfortable) that all teachers will recognise. It means *terrible*. However, the writer of the second example has tried to avoid using such a strong and emotive adjective, while nonetheless making clear their concerns.

5. <u>Qualifying modifiers.</u> *Somewhat* is a very useful word. If the writer had said 'his manner can be *a little bit* alienating', it would sound more polite but it would also lessen the force of the accusation. The beauty of adding the modifier *somewhat* to an adjective is that it sounds more polite and measured but it doesn't actually reduce the force of it at all!

As we discussed in the last chapter (page 155), you can also use the subjunctive mood to make writing more formal.

Formal and informal are not the only types of register. When we talk about a piece of writing being sarcastic, romantic, funny, ironic, abusive or tongue-in-cheek, we are making a remark about register. There is even a specific register for footballers' post-match interviews in which they use the present perfect tense to discuss events in the game that are now in the past:

Yeah, so I've seen Crouchy early doors. He's made the run and I've knocked it up to him. He's seen it, got on the end of it and, fortunately, it's gone in.

A grammar book is not the place to learn how to adopt every possible register we can imagine. It would be good, though, especially with older children whose understanding of grammar is quite secure, to ask them to try to identify the features of different registers themselves in their own reading.

Teaching ideas

All of the content covered in this chapter is from the Key Stage 2 curriculum, so these activities are pitched at children in Year 3 to Year 6. For teaching ideas on adverbials, head to Chapter 12, page 123.

Miss Boardmarker's school trip

This is a fantastic activity for teaching formal and informal register. Miss Scarlett Boardmarker is a primary school teacher. She has taken her class on a school trip to a sweet factory, where they have had a rubbish day. Miss Boardmarker has written two letters about her day. One was to Mr Booker, a teacher from another school who was also thinking about taking his class to the sweet factory. He wanted to know what Miss Boardmarker thought about the trip. The other letter was to her friend Jemma, telling her what a rubbish day she'd had. Read both the letters with your class (you'll find them below and also as digital versions in the online resources for you to print or display on a whiteboard). Then, using the letters, challenge your class to answer the following questions. You can add your own questions if you wish!

1. What is the name of the town Miss Boardmarker's school is in?
2. List three things that went wrong when Miss Boardmarker's class went to the sweet factory.
3. Do you think Mr Booker is a close friend of Miss Boardmarker? Explain your answer.
4. Which of the two letters did Miss Boardmarker write first? How do you know?
5. Do you think Miss Boardmarker has a well-behaved class? Explain your answer.
6. Do you think Miss Boardmarker is young or old? Why?
7. How do you think Miss Boardmarker knows her friend Jemma? Explain your answer.
8. Explain why everyone was disappointed to be given a free bookmark at the sweet factory.
9. List three features of the letter to Mr Booker that show that it is a formal letter.
10. List three features of the letter to Jemma that show that it is an informal letter.

Miss Boardmarker's formal letter to the teacher asking whether the trip was worthwhile

Lennon Park Primary School
Dawson Road
Woodgate
WG61 1TH

Dear Mr Booker,

I am writing in response to your letter enquiring about our class visit to the sweet factory last week. Obviously, the children were excited to be going to the sweet factory and I expected that they would learn a great deal about how sweets are made and about how factories work. I am sorry to say, however, that the day was neither as enjoyable nor as educational as I might have hoped.

When we first arrived, there was nobody at the entrance to meet us. As a result, the children and adults in our group were left waiting for over half an hour with nothing to do. Despite our best efforts to keep the children entertained, the unexpected wait made it difficult to keep their behaviour under control.

When we were eventually invited into the factory, we were taken on a guided tour. The member of staff who led the tour did not always explain things very clearly and he did not seem particularly comfortable talking to the children. He attempted to explain the functions of the different machines but even I could not always understand what he meant, so I imagine the children found it very difficult indeed to follow what he was saying.

Despite it being a sweet factory, we did not actually see any sweets at all. Their leaflet clearly stated that the children would be given a 'free gift' at the end of the day. You can imagine their disappointment when this turned out to be a bookmark with the factory logo printed on it.

For these reasons, I am afraid I cannot recommend the sweet factory for your next school trip. I suggest you look into other possibilities. I trust that you will find this information helpful.

Yours sincerely,

S Boardmarker

Miss S Boardmarker

Miss Boardmarker's informal letter to her friend about the trip

Hi Jemma,

Hope you're OK. How's things? I've had such a rubbish day today. We went on a school trip to this sweet factory a few miles away from our school and it was a complete waste of time. We got there at half past nine and there was nobody to meet us. I had to stand around for about half an hour trying to stop the snotty little kids in my class from killing each other out of boredom! Honestly, we were so <u>BORED</u>!!!

When we finally went in, we were shown round the factory by this boring old fart who must have been about 100 years old. He waffled on about heaven knows what for well over an hour and none of us could understand a word he said. He was a bit like Mr Griffiths, that dinosaur who taught us history for GCSE. Do you remember him? It seemed like this guy had been dead for years! I don't think he'd ever met a child before. He didn't have a clue how to speak to them. They were bored out of their tiny little minds!

If all that wasn't bad enough, the 'free gift' we'd been promised turned out to be a bookmark. Can you believe that? A bookmark! It's a SWEET FACTORY for crying out loud! Would it kill them to actually give out some <u>SWEETS</u>?!!

The whole thing was awful. I am never going back there ever again. I would sooner have my eyeballs chewed out by a diseased squirrel.

Anyway, I'm rambling on. Let me know how things are with you.

See you soon. Take it easy.

Scarlett

LKS2 **UKS2**

Rewrite the school newsletter

Most schools have a weekly newsletter they send out to parents. It is an example of formal writing that the children will be familiar with. Once they understand the difference between informal and formal register, challenge your class to rewrite a section of the newsletter in an informal tone. They'll have a lot of fun with this. Well, as much fun as you can have with formal and informal voices.

 LKS2 **UKS2**

Model paragraphs

We thought long and hard about ideas for teaching paragraphs. All the suggestions we have put in the book we have used ourselves with our own classes over the years. When we think about how we have taught paragraphs, it hasn't been with a worksheet, a quiz or a game. It hasn't even been by showing pupils paragraphs in books (although that was part of it). The two things we've done that have helped our pupils understand how and where to use paragraphs are: teaching them to plan their texts and modelling using paragraphs with the class. Before they write anything, we usually do some modelled or shared writing on the board. This is the time to discuss where the paragraphs are going to go and more importantly WHY. Model your thought process aloud to the class: *'OK, so the next bit of the story is going to be in the garden rather than in the kitchen so I think I will start a new paragraph now. Can anyone suggest an appropriate adverbial to start the first sentence of this new paragraph?'*

 LKS2 **UKS2**

Planning paragraphs

This works better when writing a non-fiction text, e.g. if your pupils are writing about why some women were given the vote in 1918. They might start off planning with a simple spider diagram as follows:

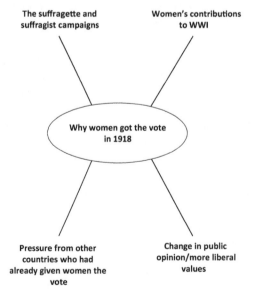

Here you have four main points, each of which will require at least one paragraph. From this point, you might want to provide your pupils with a planning sheet like the one below to help them expand the points into paragraphs. There is a printable copy of this sheet in the online resources.

Planning sheet

Paragraph 1	
Main point:	Supporting ideas/analysis/evidence, etc.
Paragraph 2	
Main point:	Supporting ideas/analysis/evidence, etc.
Paragraph 3	
Main point:	Supporting ideas/analysis/evidence, etc.
Paragraph 4	
Main point:	Supporting ideas/analysis/evidence, etc.

Spot the cohesive devices

LKS2

UKS2

Look at the extract below and read it as a class. Give each child a copy of the text (there is a printable version in the online resources) and ask them to try to spot some of the cohesive devices they have been learning about. Discuss what effect these devices have on the text. Why are they necessary? What would the text be like without them?

Extract

Poppy was a contented girl. She had wonderful friends, a cosy and comfortable home and a family who wouldn't have looked out of place in *The Waltons*. Yes, Poppy was a very happy child. However, there was one thing Poppy didn't have: a pet. Oh, how she longed for a fluffy companion, a furry friend. Everywhere she looked, Poppy saw pets: dogs walking on leads down the street, cats staring out of living room windows and rabbits chewing grass in the front garden. It simply wasn't fair.

Chapter 18

Breaking the 'rules'

Chapter overview

Now the real fun can start! In this chapter we will look at:

• The origins of words and how etymology affects grammar.	UKS2	Pages 171–172
• The boundaries between word classes and the way individual words can cut across them.	UKS2	Pages 172–173
• How to incorporate non-sentences into a piece of writing.	UKS2	Pages 173–174
• Ideas and resources to support teaching of these concepts.	UKS2	Pages 174–175

As you'll be well aware by now, throughout this book, we've avoided talking about grammar *rules*. This is because there is no such thing. We have tried to avoid using words like *should* and *must* to describe grammatical conventions. Rules have to be set and enforced by someone and there is, thankfully, no such body in the English-speaking world. The conventions explained in this book are not regulations you are forced to obey. They merely provide information about how people do, in fact, tend to write. You will be able to find exceptions and counterexamples for almost everything that we've said before – and many of your pupils will too. Grammar is not maths. To say that multiples of five must end in a five or a zero is to invoke a universal truth and there are no counterexamples. To say that question marks go at the end of questions simply isn't that sort of truth – it's just a description of most people's current writing behaviour.

For that reason, we thought it would be worth ending our journey through the basics of English grammar by celebrating some of the ways the rules can be broken, and why this is often no bad thing.

Etymology and made-up words

All words are made up. Every single one. At some point, they didn't exist, and then they did. They weren't delivered to a great prophet of grammar on stone tablets in ancient times. They just happened. People said things, other people knew what they meant, and those utterances became words. The words *bandit, critic, lonely, dauntless* and *dwindle* were all invented by Shakespeare. In fact, he invented over 1,700 words used in the English language.

Sometimes a completely new sound can come to be associated with a particular thing but, more often, words have a story. Consider the word *meme*. The word was first coined by evolutionary biologist Richard Dawkins in the 1970s to describe any idea, behaviour or style that spreads from person to person within a culture. He took the Ancient Greek word *mimeme*, meaning 'imitated thing', and shortened it to sound like the word *gene*. He used this new word to demonstrate how ideas can spread and reproduce in a similar manner to the way genes do. At some point more than 40 years later, someone used this word to describe, very specifically, a familiar picture (be it confident Buzz Lightyear with his arm around an overwhelmed Woodie, Leonardo DiCaprio brandishing a martini glass or the distracted boyfriend looking at the girl in the red dress) annotated with text being widely circulated on social media. This story of a word's origins is called its <u>etymology</u> and it's a fascinating topic. Most words in our language were formed by a succession of invaders 1,000 to 2,000 years ago: Romans, Saxons, Vikings and Normans. Ancient Latin, Germanic and Scandinavian languages were hammered together in a haphazard fashion to form the rudiments of English. In the global age we now live in, and partly due to some rather embarrassing and somewhat shameful incidents in the colonial era, our language has influences from all over the world. Many mathematical terms like *algebra* and *algorithm* came to us via Arabic, the word *chocolate* comes from the Aztecs and, believe it or not, the word *bungalow* entered the English language via Hindi.

However, as we've said a number of times now, the purpose of grammar is to make sense – to make ourselves understood by other people. If we're going to make up words or adopt them from other languages, we have to do it in such a way that other people will understand what we're talking about. The Year 6 grammar test isn't the time for children to make up their own words but there's no harm in letting them do it from time to time, especially if they can find a creative and meaningful way to do it, such that their reader is able to understand what they're saying.

Changing word classes

The word *elbow* was first used as a verb by Shakespeare ('A sovereign shame so elbows him' – *King Lear*). Before that, it had only ever functioned as a noun. One of the interesting ways in which we can break grammatical 'rules' without noticing is to change the class of a word due to the way we use it. Consider the way *Google* has become a verb as well as a proper noun over the last 20 years. Sometimes this might involve simply using the word in an unusual way:

That is so him.

People say this sort of thing a lot. They mean that something he (whoever he is) has done is typical of his behaviour. Alternatively, it may mean that a particular item of clothing really suits him. What is intriguing is that *him* functions not as a pronoun in this sentence as it usually would, but as an adjective.

Sometimes, we create new words by adding a suffix associated with a particular word class to the end. You'll sometimes hear people say something like:

Don't go that way; it's really <u>trafficky</u>.

We know what they mean and they've made the noun *traffic* into an adjective by adding a *-y* suffix. We can even make a judgement about how to spell it by comparing it to similar real words that have an optional *-y* suffix (e.g. *panic – panicky*). Here are some other examples:

I'm worried that our politics is getting <u>Trumpified</u> by social media.
(A noun has been turned into a verb.)

My breakfast this morning was not very <u>Instagrammable</u>.
(A noun has been turned into an adjective.)

I <u>Googled</u> the names of Henry VIII's wives.
(A noun has been turned into a verb.)

Try making up some of your own, or encourage your pupils to. You might even find yourselves having an interesting conversation about word classes and suffixes!

Non-sentences

Throughout this book, we've concentrated on the grammar of and within <u>sentences</u>, but much of what we write isn't composed of sentences at all. We write shopping lists and take notes; we send text messages and we tweet. We certainly don't speak in grammatically coherent sentences most of the time.

Even when writing more formally, like when writing a story, we may often include non-sentences for perfectly good reasons.

Nyinka looked out of the window and listened. Nothing. Silence. She watched and waited until, all of a sudden, the church bells in the town started ringing. Every single one.

There are two sentences in the extract above and three non-sentences:

Nothing.
Silence.
Every single one.

These don't contain verbs or subjects – they're just words or phrases. They aren't sentences. But, if writing them like this helps to build suspense and tension in the extract, who cares? You may also have noticed that we started the last sentence with a coordinating conjunction – *but*. And I started this one with *and*. And this one. And do you know what? We can hear no sirens. No flashing lights. No one is coming to arrest us because there are no grammar police. There are self-appointed grammar fascists, of course – heaven knows, there are plenty of those – but more often than not they're the idiots, not you. They're the ones who don't understand how the English language works. No one makes the rules, even if the Department for Education would like to. We just have an untidy patchwork of evolved and overlapping conventions.

Good writers recognise and acknowledge those conventions but they also know when to do their own thing. Writing is intended to be read and what matters is the effect of your writing on the reader.

As for those guys who pick you up for saying *who* instead of *whom*? Their attitude just doesn't make sense. We should know. We wrote a book on making sense – and we hope you've enjoyed it.

Teaching ideas

Before you launch into rule-breaking, it is really important that your pupils are secure in their understanding of grammatical conventions and how to use them. For this reason, the teaching ideas listed below are for an upper Key Stage 2 class. However, the best thing you can do for those pupils who are ready to start breaking the rules is expose them to a wide range of reading material that provides them with examples of authors breaking the rules. You could start with the opening line to *A Christmas Carol*, for example.

UKS2 Marley was dead: to begin with

Dickens's use of a colon is quite eccentric. Read it with your pupils and discuss why he might have chosen it and what effect it has on the reader.

UKS2 Make your own rules

Once you've introduced your pupils to the idea that new words can be created by adding a suffix to a noun to change the word class, e.g. Googled, Trumpified and so on, challenge them to come up with their own. Remind them that the root word has to be familiar enough that everybody understands what is implied by this new word. Once they have had time to generate their new words, see whether the rest of the class can work out what the meaning of their new word is.

UKS2 Write your own Jabberwocky

Lewis Carroll invented plenty of nonsense words in his time. Have a look at the opening stanza of his poem, 'Jabberwocky':

> `Twas brillig, and the slithy toves
> Did gyre and gimble in the wabe:
> All mimsy were the borogoves,
> And the mome raths outgrabe.

What's interesting about this is that although there are a number of nonsense words, they are used in a way that is grammatically correct – it makes sense to the reader. To start with, try getting your pupils to write a translation of this stanza. They could then come up with their own mythical creature and use nonsense words to write their own poem.

Non-sentences

Introduce your pupils to the 'non-sentence'. As we mentioned earlier, it's really important that they understand what a sentence is before you get to this. Give them a few examples (see below if you need some inspiration) and discuss them as a class. Point out that these sorts of sentences are used to build tension or suspense and are often just one or two words. Then give them time to write a few of their own.

Examples of non-sentences

Jemima looked up. Her brother looked different. Completely different.

Nyinka looked out of the window and listened. Nothing. Silence. She watched and waited until, all of a sudden, the church bells in the town started ringing. Every single one.

Something brushed past Jack. He shivered. It wasn't something. It was someone. Him. He didn't know it at the time but that was the last time he would see his friend. Alive.

Appendices

Appendices

Appendix 1

Word classes and word families

Most words in English sentences can be categorised according to eight broad <u>word classes</u>. Here is a list of the word classes and where you can find more information about them:

Nouns	– Chapter 2, page 24
Pronouns	– Chapter 3, page 34
Determiners	– Chapter 3, page 37
Verbs	– Chapter 4, page 46
Adjectives	– Chapter 6, page 64
Adverbs	– Chapter 6, page 69
Prepositions	– Chapter 11, page 112
Conjunctions	– Chapter 11, page 113

It must be emphasised that individual words are not fixed within any of these categories. Most words can have different classes depending on how they are used in the sentence:

Nina <u>likes</u> cheese.	**likes** is a verb
What are your <u>likes</u> and dislikes?	**likes** is a noun
<u>That</u> is a good idea.	**That** is a pronoun
<u>That</u> pencil is mine.	**That** is a determiner
Run <u>for</u> the hills.	**for** is a preposition
Have courage <u>for</u> we are many.	**for** is a conjunction
You took that corner too <u>fast</u>.	**fast** is an adverb
Cheetahs are <u>fast</u>.	**fast** is an adjective

Many words have several different <u>inflections,</u> or versions, that give you a clue as to the word class within which they are acting in a particular context. These are called word families, e.g.:

Education is usually a noun.	**Defiance** is usually a noun.
Educate is usually a verb.	**Defy** is usually a verb.
Educational is usually an adjective.	**Defiant** is usually an adjective.
Educationally is usually an adverb.	**Defiantly** is usually an adverb.

Sometimes there can be different inflections for the same word class within the same word family with subtly different meanings. For example, *memorial* and *memory* are usually both nouns within the word family that includes other inflections such as *memorable* and *memorise*.

The inflection that indicates the word class is often determined by the suffix at the end of a word. For a long time, teachers taught adverbs as *-ly* words but, in reality, the words most often used as adverbs (e.g. *well, again, today, now*) don't end in *-ly* and many words that aren't adverbs do:

We can't rely on our cowardly ally.

In this sentence, *rely* is a verb, *cowardly* is an adjective and *ally* is a noun. Please don't teach children that adverbs are *-ly* words. It isn't true.

However, if you want to teach children about suffixes that do help them to guess the word class of a particular word, you have a glorious grammatical smorgasbord of options, especially when it comes to nouns and adjectives. A word ending in *-ation,* for example, is very likely to be a noun. Where it isn't a noun, it's likely to be derived from one (e.g. when *ration* is used as a verb). Here are some more suffixes that indicate a word is likely, but not guaranteed, to be a noun:

-age -ance -ence -dom -hood -ism -ity -ment -ness -ship -sion -tion

You will no doubt be able to think of exceptions for most of them but these are useful patterns to point out to children. By the same token, there are several suffixes that are likely, but not guaranteed, to indicate adjectives:

-able -ible -ful -ic -ish -ive -ian -less -ous

In general, however, there are no shortcuts to teaching children to identify different word classes. They need to be able to identify the word's role in the sentence and work out from there which of the eight categories it fits into best.

Appendix 2
Phrasal verbs

Phrasal verbs are incredibly common in English and, if you are able to read this book, it's safe to assume you use them all the time without noticing. They are verb phrases in which a verb is combined with a conjunction to create a new verb form with a meaning slightly different from either of its original components. There are too many to list them all but here are just a few:

I need to <u>pick up</u> my children.

These clothes need to be <u>put away</u>.

Muhammad <u>found out</u> the truth.

Let's <u>carry on</u>.

Don't <u>give up</u>.

We've <u>run out</u> of milk.

Freya <u>caught up</u> with her friends.

Stop <u>showing off</u>.

Once you notice phrasal verbs for the first time, you wonder how you've never noticed them before. They are everywhere in English and they are a nightmare for non-native speakers of our language, since every combination has a unique meaning. For this reason, it's a really good idea to draw children's attention to them, especially if English isn't spoken at home. In all of the examples above, the phrasal verb acts as the main verb phrase in the sentence. You may have noticed that some of these sentences have an object (and wouldn't make sense if they didn't) whereas some have no object. That is to say, some of them are transitive whereas some of them are intransitive (see Appendix 3, page 183). Some of them even have one meaning in their transitive form and a completely different meaning in their intransitive form! Take a look at these examples:

Saadia <u>made up</u> a story.

After their argument, David and Subir <u>made up</u>.

If all of this wasn't confusing enough for somebody learning English as an additional language, many of our phrasal verbs can be split up, with the verb on one side of a noun or noun phrase, and the preposition on the other:

Don't <u>mess</u> this <u>up</u>.

Who <u>threw</u> my sandwich <u>away</u>?

Bella <u>turned</u> the lights <u>off</u>.

In all of these examples, the verb acts as the main verb in the sentence while the preposition acts as an object complement (see Appendix 5, page 189). Phrasal verb, like so much in grammar, is a complicated term for something very simple – but something we can easily neglect to mention to our pupils.

Appendix 3
Transitive and intransitive verbs

Don't panic about this one! It's actually pretty simple. A <u>transitive verb</u> is a verb that must have an object or a complement to complete it. Consider these non-sentences:

~~I bring.~~

~~Eleanor takes.~~

~~They send.~~

These verbs are incomplete because they lack an object. Grammatically speaking, you have to bring *something* to somewhere. You have to take *something* (unless you're deliberately using the verb in an unusual stylistic manner, e.g. *'You know your problem? You just take and you take and you take.'*) You have to send *something*.

    <u>Intransitive verbs</u>, by comparison, are those that do not require an object or a complement to complete them:

Tottenham <u>won</u>.

Did you <u>resign</u>?

Mr Weller <u>died</u>.

In all of these examples, the intransitive verbs complete the sentence on their own. We've included this distinction in this book because it appears in the National Curriculum for Key Stage 2. We're not convinced it's a particularly important concept to teach primary school children but there are cases where it might be a helpful way to clarify misconceptions in children's writing, especially for children with English as an additional language.

Appendix 4

Finite verbs, infinitives and participles

<u>Finite verbs</u> are the main verbs in <u>finite clauses</u>. They appear alongside a subject in a sentence and they are written in one specific simple tense:

I <u>like</u> cheese   Simple present tense

Kim <u>spoke</u> to Rob   Simple past tense

To understand what makes these verbs finite, we need to take a look at their opposite, <u>non-finite verbs</u>, of which there are two main sorts: <u>infinitives</u> and <u>participles</u>.

All verbs apart from modal verbs have an <u>infinitive form</u>, which you might want to think of as the general or generic form of the verb, beginning with the word *to*, e.g. *to run, to talk, to find*. Infinitive forms are used when you want to talk about carrying out the action denoted by the verb in a general sense, without a specific tense:

I like <u>to walk</u> my dog.

In this example, one infers from the author's words that they have walked their dog in the past and will do so again in the future. For all we know, they may even be walking their dog right now! The verb *like* is written in the present tense – it is finite. But the infinitive form *to walk* is general; it has no tense. This idea is relatively simple in English, as the infinitive form is usually just the first-person, present-tense form of the verb with the word *to* in front of it:

I go *(first person, simple present)*   **To go** *(infinitive)*

I believe *(first person, simple present)*   **To believe** *(infinitive)*

I defenestrate *(first person, simple present)*   **To defenestrate** *(infinitive)*

There is one total exception to the above rule and unfortunately it's probably the most common verb in our language:

I am *(first person, simple present)*   **To be** *(infinitive)*

Children find it quite hard to understand that *to be* is the same verb as *I am* and all its many other wildly irregular forms (*we are, it is, she was, they were*, etc.) but it's quite an important aspect of English grammar, especially when it comes to understanding how auxiliary verbs work (see Chapter 4, page 47). The more a word is used in a language, perhaps unfortunately, the more it gets warped and altered by the centuries.

The other type of non-finite verb is the participle, which we touched on a little bit in Chapter 4, page 48. There are two kinds: the present participle and the past participle.

Present participles are the form of the verb that ends in *-ing*:

Stop being so silly!

In this command, or imperative, the verb *stop* is finite. However, the phrase *being so silly* refers to the act of being silly generally; it doesn't have its own tense. Present participles are often used to talk about doing things *generally*, rather than at a particular time:

Talking to his parents, you realise why he is the way he is.
I will miss having these chats when you go to your new school.
Sitting down for too long is supposed to be bad for your back.

The rules for adding the *-ing* suffix are relatively simple: in most cases, you just add it and get on with your life. However, English being English, there are of course a couple of exceptions:

1. If the infinitive form of the verb ends in a consonant followed by an *e* (e.g. *have, bake, hope*), you take off the *e* and then add the suffix (e.g. *having, baking, hoping*).
2. Furthermore, if the infinitive form of the verb ends in a vowel followed by *any single consonant apart from y* (e.g. *sit, bet, rot*), you double that final consonant before adding the suffix (e.g. *sitting, betting, rotting*).

Past participles are a little less predictable but they usually end either in *-d, -ed, -n, -ne* or *-en*. You can identify the past participle for any given verb by working out which form of it would follow the words *I have* when forming the present perfect tense:

To do – I have done
To have – I have had
To stop – I have stopped
To try – I have tried
To be – I have been
To go – I have gone/been

Both present and past participles can be used with auxiliary verbs to form different tenses (see Chapter 4, page 47) but the tense is determined by the form of auxiliary verb used, not the choice of participle:

I had done	Past perfect
I have done	Present perfect
I will have done	Future perfect

All three of these tenses uses the past participle of *done*. However, one is a type of past tense, one is a type of present tense and the other is a type of future tense: this is determined by the form of the finite auxiliary verb *to have* that has been chosen. Present participles have the same versatility:

I was going	Past progressive
I am going	Present continuous
I will be going	Future continuous

Appendix 5
Complements and adjuncts

Complements

A common mistake for teachers and pupils is confusing objects with <u>complements</u>. Often the purpose of a sentence is to give the reader or listener information about the subject. In these instances, the sentence is likely to include a <u>subject complement</u>: a word or phrase that completes the verb and tells you more about the subject. It is not a separate person or thing, and therefore a complement is different from an object, but it can often be found in the same part of the sentence. For example:

Mr Pearson became <u>a teacher</u>.
Ajarni was feeling <u>very bored</u>.
You look <u>wonderful</u>.

Notice that the verbs in these sentences wouldn't make sense (or would at least have a completely different meaning) if you took the subject complements away. A subject complement is different from an object because it only gives you information about the subject – it doesn't tell you about anyone or anything else.

Just as subject complements complete the verb and give us more information about the subject, <u>object complements</u> complete the verb and give us more information about (you guessed it) the object. To be precise, they usually give us more information about the manner in which the object has been affected by the verb. They almost always appear at the end of the sentence or clause. Here are some examples:

The sorcerer turned the prince <u>into a frog</u>.
My friends make me <u>happy</u>.
Defeat in battle made a bad situation <u>even worse</u>.

Notice that, like subject complements, object complements can be individual words or longer phrases. The verb phrase in each sentence only makes sense because the object complement is there to complete its meaning.

Adjuncts

What about the 'other bits' of simple sentences? What about those words or phrases that are neither subject nor object, verb phrase nor complement? All of these other elements are called <u>adjuncts</u> and they are often adverbial in nature. That is to say, they are often adverbs or adverbial phrases and they describe the manner, time, place, degree, frequency or intensity with which the action described in the sentence takes place. Here are a few examples:

<u>On Sundays,</u> we <u>sometimes</u> visit grandma.
That man <u>often</u> seems to be staring at something <u>across the road</u>.
<u>In all honesty,</u> I think I may have misjudged the situation <u>completely</u>.

What we can take away from all of this is that there is nothing simple about simple sentences! A simple sentence may only contain one clause, but that clause can involve detailed subjects and objects, complex verb phrases, complements and adjuncts. Here are some examples of simple sentences that are, well, really quite complicated!

My first day at the new school surely had to be one of the most difficult days of my entire life.
> Subject: *My first day at the new school*
> Verb phrase: *had to be*
> Subject complement: *one of the most difficult days of my entire life*
> Adjunct: *surely*

The previous Saturday morning, Cynthia's eldest daughter had decided to send her a long and detailed email full of hurtful accusations.
> Subject: *Cynthia's eldest daughter*
> Verb phrase: *had decided to send*
> Direct object: *a long and detailed email full of hurtful accusations*
> Indirect object: *her (Cynthia)*
> Adjunct: *The previous Saturday morning*

Luckily for the vice-chairman of the company, his unscrupulous business associates had already decided, somewhat reluctantly, to give him his rightful share of the money back.
> Subject: *his unscrupulous business associates*
> Verb phrase: *had already decided to give him*
> Direct object: *his rightful share of the money*
> Indirect object: *him (the vice-chairman of the company)*
> Object complement: *back*
> Adjunct: *Luckily for the vice-chairman of the company; somewhat reluctantly*

Appendix 6

Dummy subjects and implied subjects

Read this sentence and ask yourself where the subject is:

It is easy to get confused by all these grammatical terms.

Stumped? You're not alone. It's quite common for sentences to contain what's known as a <u>dummy subject</u>, usually either *it* or *there*. This might start to make a little more sense if you ask yourself what or whom the word *it* refers to in the above example. The answer is nothing! It has no semantic content at all – it refers to no one in particular but merely stands in for the subject in the way that a shop window dummy stands in for a real person wearing a dress. A similar phenomenon is at work here:

There was a terrible fire.

Once again, the word *there* has no semantic content of its own; it merely fills the role of the subject in the sentence. Sentences like this are remarkably common and, when teaching children to find the subject of a sentence, you may be asked about them.

You will also find that some sentences have an implied subject. This is particularly common for commands, also known as <u>imperatives</u> (see Chapter 16, page 154, for more on these). Consider this sentence:

Give me that!

This sentence contains a verb, an indirect object and a direct object but there is no subject in sight. However, it is obvious who the subject is from the context. If someone were to say this to you, you would be in no doubt that *you* were the person expected to act and therefore you would be the subject! Although it is not stated, it is very heavily *implied*. You will also find implied subjects in some subordinate clauses, especially participle clauses. Here is an example:

<u>Having fully assessed the terrible extent of the flood damage</u>, Ryan phoned his insurance company.

In the example above, the subject of the fronted participle clause is not stated outright, but it's completely obvious from the main clause that the person who assessed the flood damage was Ryan.

The other place where locating the subject can be tricky is in questions, otherwise known as interrogative clauses:

<u>Where</u> is my hat?

<u>What</u> are you doing?

<u>Who</u> stole my cheese?

In all the questions above, the underlined <u>interrogative pronoun</u> (or 'question word' if you like) is the subject of the sentence. This can be a little bit counterintuitive but, as with all pronouns, these words are standing in for particular nouns or noun phrases (it's just that the person asking these questions doesn't yet know which ones!).

Appendix 7
Discourse markers

A lot of resources and sources of information will refer to 'discourse markers'. These are found in almost all types of writing but they are especially numerous in non-fiction texts. They organise, separate and introduce *segments of spoken or written discourse* (points or ideas). They can be individual words or longer phrases and they can fall into different word classes. For example, *and* when used as a *conjunction*, *equally* when used as an *adverb* and *following* when used as a *verb* can all be deployed as discourse markers. Some of them would go at the start of a sentence whereas others would have to go in the middle, supported by other words or phrases.

In spoken language, discourse markers are those little phrases that link our remarks together and knit them into coherent conversations, e.g.:

Well, I mean…

Now that you mention it…

But don't you think…

In written grammar, they link sentences, clauses and paragraphs together and help to provide cohesion to the whole text (see Chapter 17, page 163, for more on cohesive devices). You may find it useful to provide your pupils with banks of discourse markers when they're writing. It's probably what those well-meaning teachers were trying to do in the last decade when they baffled their pupils with incoherent nonsense about 'connectives'.

Here are ten types of discourse markers that you might want to share with your pupils. You'll notice there's some overlap between the lists of examples. You're a primary school teacher so you'll probably want to make them into a pretty chart and laminate it or something. Yeah, we see you.

1. Discourse markers to begin your writing

    These words and phrases begin your first point, event, idea or argument. The style of discourse marker you go for will depend on the task in hand.

    Examples: *firstly, to begin with, at the beginning, in the first instance, for one thing, initially, at the start, primarily, originally.*

2. Discourse markers for adding to and supporting a previous remark

These are words or phrases that add information or ideas to previous comments. They're particularly useful for introducing a new point or piece of argument to build up one side of an argument.

Examples: *and, furthermore, moreover, in addition, then, also, besides, too, again.*

3. Discourse markers for sequencing information, events and ideas

These are what, in the past, you may have called 'time connectives' – an unhelpful word to use for all the reasons outlined in Chapter 11, page 111. They indicate orders, sequences or chronology.

Examples: *firstly, secondly, thirdly, finally, then, next, meanwhile, before, during, while, whilst, after, subsequently, eventually.*

4. Discourse markers for illustrating and exemplifying

These introduce examples and clarifications that support a point you've just been making or make it clearer to your reader what you mean.

Examples: *for example, such as, for instance, as you can see from, illustrated by, as demonstrated when, in the case of.*

5. Discourse markers for comparing

These link one idea to a similar idea or another example that demonstrates the same point.

Examples: *similarly, likewise, as with, just as, like, equally, in the same way.*

6. Discourse markers for contrasting

These are the opposite of discourse markers for comparing. They link one idea that is not the same or they might link a piece of evidence for one point of view to another piece of evidence that considers a different point of view.

Examples: *but, yet, whereas, despite, alternatively, on the other hand, conversely, having said that, nevertheless, however, notwithstanding.*

7. Discourse markers for qualifying

These discourse markers tend to introduce exceptions or limitations to the point or idea before them, encouraging the reader to treat it with caution in some way, rather than assuming it is always applicable.

Examples: *except, apart from, unless, providing, as long as, if, although, albeit, provided that.*

8. Discourse markers for establishing cause and effect

These words and phrases make it clear that one state of affairs is responsible for another state of affairs. Some (like *because*) require the effect to be explained before the discourse marker and the cause afterwards. Others (like *therefore*) work the other way around: they require the cause to be explained before the discourse marker and the effect afterwards.

Examples: *because, as a result of, consequently, owing to, due to, thus, therefore, ergo.*

9. Discourse markers for emphasising

These indicate that the point or idea following them is particularly important compared to other points or ideas that have been stated.

Examples: *above all, in particular, primarily, especially, critically, most importantly, significantly, indeed, notably.*

10. Discourse markers for concluding and summarising

These often introduce the final point in a piece of writing. They tend to indicate that the discourse is coming to an end and they tend to introduce a recap of its main point.

Examples: *finally, to conclude, ultimately, on the whole, overall, in general, to summarise, basically, in short, in the end, when it comes down to it.*

Glossary

Need a quick, at-a-glance definition? Here is our edited and abridged version of the Department for Education (2013b) glossary that shows the technical grammatical terms used in the National Curriculum. We've added a few of our own and linked every concept to the chapters in this book. Need more information? Head to the relevant page number for further information about the concept, as well as teaching ideas and resources.

Term	Definition	Page
Active voice	An active <u>verb</u> has its usual pattern of <u>subject</u> and <u>object</u> (in contrast with the <u>passive</u>).	156
Adjective	A word that modifies a noun. The surest way to identify adjectives is by the ways they can be used: • before a noun, to make the noun's meaning more specific (i.e. to modify the noun), or • after the verb *be*, as its complement. Adjectives are sometimes called 'describing words' because they pick out single characteristics such as size or colour.	64
Adverb	Adverbs can modify a verb, an adjective, another adverb or even a whole clause.	69
Adverbial	An adverbial is a word or phrase that is used, like an adverb, to modify a verb or clause. Of course, <u>adverbs</u> can be used as adverbials, but many other types of words and phrases can be used this way, including <u>prepositional phrases</u> and <u>subordinate clauses</u>.	71
Apostrophe	Apostrophes have two completely different uses: 1. showing the place of missing letters, e.g. *I'm* for *I am* 2. showing ownership, e.g. *Tim's pen*.	78
Article	The articles *the* (definite) and *a* or *an* (indefinite) are the most common type of <u>determiner</u>.	39
Auxiliary verb	The <u>auxiliary verbs</u> are: *be, have, do* and the <u>modal verbs</u>. They can be used to make questions and negative statements. In addition: • *be* is used in the <u>progressive</u> and <u>passive</u> • *have* is used in the <u>perfect</u>. *Do* is used to form questions and negative statements if no other auxiliary verb is present.	47

Term	Definition	Page
Clause	A clause is a type of phrase that contains a verb and contains or clearly refers to a subject. Clauses can sometimes be complete sentences. Clauses may be main or subordinate.	98
Complement	A verb's subject complement adds more information about its subject, and its object complement does the same for its object. Unlike the verb's object, its complement may be an adjective. The verb *be* normally has a complement.	189
Conjunction	A conjunction links two words or phrases together. There are two main types of conjunction: 1. Coordinating conjunctions, e.g. *and*, link two words or phrases together as an equal pair. 2. Subordinating conjunctions, e.g. *when*, introduce a subordinate clause.	113
Determiner	A determiner specifies a noun as known or unknown, and it goes before any modifiers (e.g. adjectives or other nouns). Some examples of determiners are: • articles (*the*, *a* or *an*) • demonstratives (e.g. *this*, *those*) • possessives (e.g. *my*, *your*) • quantifiers (e.g. *some*, *every*).	37
Direct speech	Direct speech is the reporting of speech by repeating the actual words of a speaker, demarcated with speech marks or quotation marks. For example: *'It has been a privilege to work with you for these last ten years,' said the headteacher.*	144
Ellipsis	Ellipsis is the omission of a word or phrase that is expected and predictable.	91
Finite verb	Every sentence typically has at least one verb that is in either the past or the present tense. Such verbs are called 'finite'. The imperative verb in a command is also finite. Verbs that are not finite, such as participles or infinitives, cannot stand on their own: they are linked to another verb in the sentence.	185
Fronted/fronting	A word or phrase that normally comes after the <u>verb</u> may be moved before the verb: when this happens, we say it has been 'fronted'. For example, a fronted adverbial is an <u>adverbial</u> that has been moved before the verb. When writing fronted phrases, we often follow them with a comma.	71

Term	Definition	Page
Infinitive	A verb's infinitive is the basic form used as the head-word in a dictionary (e.g. *walk, be*). Infinitives are often used: • after *to* • after <u>modal verbs</u>.	185
Intransitive verb	A verb that does not need an object in a sentence to complete its meaning is described as intransitive. See '<u>transitive verb</u>'.	183
Main clause	A main clause is a grammatical construction that expresses meaning: it describes a relationship, a circumstance or a state of affairs. It always includes a verb or a verb phrase and it usually includes a subject too. A main clause can be a sentence without a subordinate clause.	98
Modal verb	Modal verbs are used to change the meaning of other <u>verbs</u>. They can express meanings such as certainty, ability or obligation. The main modal verbs are *will, would, can, could, may, might, shall, should, must* and *ought*. A modal verb only has <u>finite</u> forms and has no <u>suffixes</u> (e.g. *I sing – he sings*, but not *I must – he musts*).	50
Modifier	One word or phrase modifies another by making its meaning more specific. Because the two words make a <u>phrase</u>, the 'modifier' is normally close to the modified word.	64
Noun	The surest way to identify nouns is by the ways they can be used after <u>determiners</u> such as *the*: for example, most nouns will fit into the frame 'The __ matters/matter.' Nouns are sometimes called 'naming words' because they name people, places and 'things'. Nouns may be classified as **common** (e.g. *boy, day*) or **proper** (e.g. *Ivan, Wednesday*), and also as **countable** (e.g. *thing, boy*) or **uncountable** (e.g. *stuff, money*). These classes can be recognised by the determiners they combine with.	24
Noun phrase	A noun phrase is a <u>phrase</u> with a noun as its <u>head</u>, e.g. *some foxes, foxes with bushy tails*. Some grammarians recognise one-word phrases, so that *foxes are multiplying* would contain the noun *foxes* acting as the head of the noun phrase *foxes*.	120
Object	An object is normally a <u>noun</u>, <u>pronoun</u> or <u>noun phrase</u> that comes straight after the <u>verb</u>, and shows what the verb is acting upon. Objects can be turned into the <u>subject</u> of a <u>passive</u> verb, and cannot be <u>adjectives</u> (contrast with <u>complements</u>).	57

Term	Definition	Page
Participle	Verbs in English have two participles, called 'present participle' (e.g. *walking*, *taking*) and 'past participle' (e.g. *walked*, *taken*). Unfortunately, these terms can be confusing to learners, because they don't necessarily have anything to do with present or past time. That said, past participles are used as <u>perfects</u> (e.g. *has eaten*) and they are also used as <u>passives</u> (e.g. *was eaten*).	185
Passive	The sentence *It was eaten by our dog* is the passive of *Our dog ate it*. A passive is recognisable from: • the past <u>participle</u> form *eaten* • the normal <u>object</u> (*it*) turned into the <u>subject</u> • the normal subject (*our dog*) turned into an optional <u>prepositional phrase</u> with *by* as its <u>head</u> • the verb *be* (*was*), or some other verb such as *get*. Contrast this with <u>active</u>. A verb is not 'passive' just because it has a passive meaning: it must be the passive version of an active verb.	156
Past tense	<u>Verbs</u> in the past tense are commonly used to: • talk about the past • talk about imagined situations • make a request sound more polite. Most verbs take the <u>suffix</u> *-ed* to form their past tense, but many commonly used verbs are irregular.	47
Perfect	The perfect form of a <u>verb</u> generally calls attention to the consequences of a prior event; for example, *he has gone to lunch* implies that he is still away, in contrast with *he went to lunch*. *Had gone to lunch* takes a past time point (e.g. *when we arrived*) as its reference point and is another way of establishing time relations in a text. The perfect tense is formed by: • turning the verb into its past <u>participle inflection</u> • adding a form of the verb *have* before it. It can also be combined with the <u>progressive</u> (e.g. *he has been going*).	49
Phrase	A phrase is a group of words that are grammatically connected so that they stay together, and they expand a single word called the 'head'. The phrase is a <u>noun phrase</u> if its head is a noun, a <u>prepositional phrase</u> if its head is a preposition, and so on; but if the head is a <u>verb</u>, the phrase is called a <u>clause</u>.	120

Term	Definition	Page
Possessive	A possessive can be: • a noun followed by an apostrophe, with or without *s* • a possessive pronoun. The relation expressed by a possessive goes well beyond ordinary ideas of 'possession'. A possessive may act as a determiner.	35, 78
Preposition	A preposition links a following noun, pronoun or noun phrase to some other word in the sentence. Prepositions often describe locations or directions, but can describe other things, such as relations of time. Words like *before* or *since* can act either as prepositions or as conjunctions.	112
Prepositional phrase	A prepositional phrase has a preposition as its head followed by a noun, pronoun or noun phrase.	123
Present tense	Verbs in the present tense are commonly used to: • talk about the present • talk about the future. They may take a suffix -*s* (depending on the subject).	47
Progressive	The progressive (also known as the 'continuous') form of a verb generally describes events in progress. It is formed by combining the verb's present participle (e.g. *singing*) with a form of the verb *be* (e.g. *he was singing*). The progressive can also be combined with the perfect (e.g. *he has been singing*).	49
Pronoun	Pronouns replace nouns in a sentence. They are normally used like nouns, except that: • They are grammatically more specialised. • It is harder to modify them.	34
Relative clause	A relative clause is a special type of subordinate clause that modifies a noun. It often does this by using a relative pronoun such as *who* or *that* to refer back to that noun, though the relative pronoun *that* is often omitted. A relative clause may also be attached to a clause. In that case, the pronoun refers back to the whole clause, rather than referring back to a noun.	104
Reported speech	Sometimes called indirect speech, reported speech is a speaker's words reported in third person with the required changes of person and tense. E.g. *The man said that he was going to the party* is reported speech based on *I am going to the party*.	144

Term	Definition	Page
Sentence	A sentence contains at least one clause. The form of a sentence's main clause shows whether it is being used as a statement, a question, a command or an exclamation. A sentence may consist of a single clause or it may contain several clauses held together by subordination or coordination.	56
Subject	The subject of a verb is normally the noun, noun phrase or pronoun that names the 'do-er' or 'be-er'. The subject's normal position is: • just before the verb in a statement • just after the auxiliary verb in a question. Unlike the verb's object and complement, the subject can determine the form of the verb (e.g. *I* am, *you* are).	56
Subjunctive	In some languages, the inflections of a verb include a large range of special forms that are used typically in subordinate clauses, and are called 'subjunctives'. English has very few such forms and those it has tend to be used in rather formal styles.	155
Subordinate clause	A clause that is subordinate to some other part of the same sentence is a subordinate clause. For example, in *Having eaten her breakfast, the cat went back to sleep*, the clause *having eaten her breakfast* is subordinate. It doesn't work as a sentence on its own; it is modifying the main clause: *the cat went back to sleep*.	99
Transitive verb	A transitive verb takes at least one object in a sentence to complete its meaning, in contrast to an intransitive verb, which does not.	183
Verb	The surest way to identify verbs is by the ways they can be used: they can usually have a tense, either present or past (see also future). Verbs are sometimes called 'doing words' because many verbs name an action that someone does; while this can be a way of recognising verbs, it doesn't distinguish verbs from nouns (which can also name actions). Moreover, many verbs name states or feelings rather than actions. Verbs can be classified as auxiliary or modal; as transitive or intransitive; and as states or events.	46
Word class	Every word belongs to a word class that summarises the ways in which it can be used in grammar. The major word classes for English are: noun, verb, adjective, adverb, preposition, determiner, pronoun and conjunction. Word classes are sometimes called 'parts of speech'.	179

Adapted from Department for Education (2013b).

FAQs (or, in other words, the most commonly encountered grammar demons)

We spoke to primary school staff up and down the country (well, mainly on Twitter) to find out the most common grammar demons. Use this page as a quick crib sheet if you want a short answer, with a page reference to go to if you want further information and teaching ideas.

1. **When should I use hyphens? I just sort of make it up and hope for the best at the moment.**

   Hyphens are used to make two words into one. There are a variety of situations in which you might need to do this but the rules often aren't as hard or fast as people think. For more information head to page 18.

2. **When do I use apostrophes and why do I sometimes get confused?**

   Apostrophes are used for two purposes: to indicate possession, e.g. *the boy's coat*, or contraction, e.g. *don't* instead of *do not*. For more on this, and for more on why this can sometimes seem confusing, please see page 78.

3. **What is an adverbial? Is it the same as an adverb?**

   An adverbial is a word phrase or a clause that modifies a verb, whereas an adverb tends to be a single word. For more information on adverbial phrases see page 122, and for more information about adverbs see page 69.

4. **How many word classes are there and why do some words seem to fit into different word classes at different times?**

   There are eight word classes you need to know about if you are teaching primary grammar. Every word in the English language has a number of different uses and can change word class depending on the context. For more on this head to page 179.

5. **Its or it's? Which is it?**

   This depends on whether you are saying something belongs to it, in which case you use *its*, e.g. *the dog wagged its tail*. If you are using a contraction of *it is* then you use *it's*, e.g. *It's my birthday tomorrow*.

6. What about your and you're?

You're is a contracted form of *you are*, e.g. *You're going to miss breakfast if you don't get up soon. Your* means it belongs to you, e.g. *Don't forget your coat.* If you are having trouble, write 'You are' instead of 'You're' and see whether your sentence still makes sense! For more on this head to page 82.

7. How do I use semi-colons?

Semi-colons are used to link main clauses that are closely related and can be considered one sentence, e.g. *There was a storm last night; the grass is wet.* They can also be used to separate items in a list in certain situations. For more on this head to page 136.

8. Is it fewer or less? When do I use them and does it matter?

Whether you use *fewer* or *less* depends on whether the noun you are referring to is countable or uncountable. For uncountable nouns, e.g. *bread, water, crime,* you use *less,* and for countable nouns, e.g. *children, friends, apples,* you use *fewer,* e.g.:
I have less water than you.
There are fewer children here than there were yesterday.
For more on this turn to page 26.

9. What about who and whom?

Use *who* when it's the subject of the sentence and *whom* when it's the object of the sentence. More on this on page 59.

10. Are speech marks the same as quotation marks? I've heard that speech marks are double and quotation marks single but I'm never really sure what I'm doing.

Most of the supposed rules that you hear about this are made up and it is almost entirely a matter of personal taste. For more on this head to page 143.

11. What's the difference between a main clause and a subordinate clause?

Broadly speaking, a main clause would make sense on its own whereas a subordinate clause would depend on a main clause to make sense. More on this on page 98.

12. What's the difference between a phrase and a clause?

This one is a very fine line but, generally speaking, a clause has to have a verb and clearly refer to a subject whereas a phrase may have one or the other but doesn't actually require either.

13. What are commas actually for?

Commas offset one part of a sentence from another. They serve several functions, which are all outlined clearly in Chapter 13, page 127. None of these functions are anything to do with breathing or pausing!

14. **What is the Oxford comma?**

The Oxford comma is an optional comma between the penultimate item in a list and the coordinating conjunction at the end of the list, e.g.:
I went to the shop and I bought bananas, peanut butter, flour, and eggs.
In this sentence, the Oxford comma is between *flour* and *and*. For more on this head to page 128.

15. **Where do 'connectives' come into all this?**

Hopefully nowhere! 'Connectives' have been flying around our schools a lot during the last 20 years but they lack any real grammatical definition. Connectives have been used to refer to adverbs of time, prepositions and conjunctions to name but a few. There is an extended rant about connectives on page 111 if that's the sort of thing you're after!

16. **What are the 'rules' for using bullet points?**

Great news! There aren't any. See page 162.

17. **How many verb tenses are there?**

There are a multitude of verb tenses but there are 12 that it is probably worth you knowing about in order to teach primary school grammar. They are outlined in Chapter 4, page 48.

18. **What in the name of all that is good and decent is the 'subjunctive mood'?**

If you want to learn more about the subjunctive, we recommend you turn to page 155.

References

Carter, R. and McCarthy, M. (2006), *Cambridge Grammar of English: A Comprehensive Guide*. Cambridge: Cambridge University Press.

Dahl, R. (1980), Letter to Jay Williams. 12 February.

Department for Education (2013a), 'English Appendix 2: Vocabulary, grammar and punctuation', https://assets.publishing.service.gov.uk/government/uploads/system/uploads/attachment_data/file/335190/English_Appendix_2_-_Vocabulary_grammar_and_punctuation.pdf

Department for Education (2013b), 'Glossary for the programmes of study for English (non-statutory)', https://assets.publishing.service.gov.uk/government/uploads/system/uploads/attachment_data/file/244216/English_Glossary.pdf

Hutchins, P. (2009), *Rosie's Walk*. New York, NY: Aladdin Paperbacks.

Martin, J. M. (2004), *The Planet Without Pronouns*. New York, NY: Scholastic.

Standards and Testing Agency (2016), 'Clarification: Key stage 1 and 2 teacher assessment and moderation guidance', https://dera.ioe.ac.uk/25684/1/Clarification_key_stage_1_and_2__teacher_assessment_and_moderation_guidance.pdf

Truss, L. (2009), *Eats, Shoots and Leaves*. London: Fourth Estate.

Index